THE JET WILL FLY!

From Beale Street to 40,000 Feet and Beyond

THE JET WILL FLY!

How to Overcome the Weight of the World

JOHNNIE EDWARD "JET" JONES JR.

The author has tried to recreate events, locations, and conversations from his/her memories of them. In some instances, in order to maintain their anonymity, the author has changed the names of individuals and places. He/she may also have changed some identifying characteristics and details such as physical attributes, occupations, and places of residence.

Copyright © 2025 by Johnnie Edward Jones Jr.

All rights reserved. No part of this book may be reproduced or transmitted in any form or by any means, electronic or mechanical, including photocopying, recording, or any information storage and retrieval system, without permission in writing from the author.

ISBN: 978-1-6653-0880-9 - Paperback
ISBN: 978-1-6653-0881-6 - Hardcover
eISBN: 978-1-6653-0882-3 - eBook

These ISBNs are the property of BookLogix for the express purpose of sales and distribution of this title. The content of this book is the property of the copyright holder only. BookLogix does not hold any ownership of the content of this book and is not liable in any way for the materials contained within. The views and opinions expressed in this book are the property of the Author/Copyright holder, and do not necessarily reflect those of BookLogix.

Library of Congress Control Number: 2024921237

☉This paper meets the requirements of ANSI/NISO Z39.48-1992 (Permanence of Paper)

Scripture quotations marked "NKJV" are taken from the New King James Version®. Copyright © 1982 by Thomas Nelson. Used by permission. All rights reserved.

011625

I HUMBLY DEDICATE this book to every person of color who has been called Colored, Negro, Black, and African American, who is a descendant of valiant and resilient ancestors, and who is struggling to overcome the weight of the world. It is also dedicated to those who desire to have peace of mind. Those of you who derive inspiration from this book will serve as justification that my life has not been in vain.

I also dedicate this book to my brother and sisters in the photo below. Together, we have continued the legacy of our mother and looked after one another, as families should. Standing are Elizabeth on the left, Denise on the right, and I in the middle. Seated are Virginia on the left, Linda on the right, and Kirby in the middle. This photo was taken on Kirby's sixtieth birthday in 2007.

Additionally, this book is dedicated to my parents, Johnnie Jones and Curley Mae Jones; my wife, Alice; and all of my other family members. I love you all. Alice deserves special recognition because she has been my best friend as well as a dedicated and loving wife. I had the benefit of watching and learning valuable lessons from my mother, and siblings in particular, as the youngest of six children. Whether you know it or not, each of you provided me with a solid foundation of love and support that allowed me to be ambitious and determined to succeed.

My sons Curtis, Johnnie, and Marion and their children have given me a reason to be someone they can be proud of. And for each grandchild alive today and those who are yet to be born, this book is for you to cherish forever. Special thanks go out to all of my family members, including all of my grandchildren. My nieces Pat, Shari, Lisa, Valerie, Rene, Michelle, Allison, and Larissa also deserve recognition. You represent the daughters I never had, and I appreciate the love you have for me.

Unfortunately, Denise's only son and my wonderful nephew Jonathan Nicholas "Nick" Jones tragically lost his life in May 2000 when he was only 20 years old. Also, Shari passed away in late 2022 and she is also missed. Thanks to her sister Pat Floyd-Echols, a retired education professional, and all family members for helping me in the editing of this book. I also appreciate my nephews Joe, Bob, and Marcus for the good times we have shared. Furthermore, special recognition goes out to Bob's only son Navy Commander Robert Floyd Jr. who is the only family member to serve in the military since Joe Floyd Sr., Kirby Ragins, Joe Floyd Jr. and myself.

On my wife's side of the family, I thank my sister-in-law Karen and brother-in-law Lavon as well as all of the cousins I have shared time with. You all have taught me something or given me inspiration in some way.

I would also like to dedicate this book to those I call friend. I hope you are inspired by knowing your friendship is very much appreciated. Perhaps we were high school classmates, or we served together in the military, or we were college classmates, neighbors, coworkers, or got to know each other in some other way. Overall, you will always hold a special place in my heart and mind. Your friendship and love are most appreciated, and whatever part you played in my life helped me to overcome the weight of the world. Thanks!

Lastly, I dedicate this book to the United States Air Force. My enlistment in the Air Force began my journey into the skies and beyond. At the tender age of seventeen, I departed home and entered a world that seemed tailor-made for me. The Air Force gave me a place to live, food to eat, a place to work, expert skills, and the discipline to be a man. Furthermore, I served with some extra special people who became lifelong friends and went to faraway places that many people will never see. All in all, the Air Force taught me how to be an excellent aviator and pilot, which kept my passengers, crew members, and myself safe over many years. I shall always be eternally grateful for the opportunity to serve my country in the United States Air Force and Air Force Reserves.

CONTENTS

Foreword — xi

Introduction — xv

A Tribute to Our African American Ancestors — xix

Growing Up in Americus — 1

School Days and Childhood Memories — 11

Off to Air Force Training and Moody Air Force Base — 35

On to Atlanta and Clark College — 55

Becoming a Proud Air Force Officer and Pilot — 71

Building Flight Time — 95

From ASA to United's Friendly Skies — 109

Captain's Authority — 135

Trying to Break Glass Ceilings into Management — 157

Retirement and Beyond — 171

Establishing My Legacy — 179

Words of Wisdom — 185

This Do in Remembrance of Me — 191

Conclusion — 193

Acknowledgments — 197

Recommended Reading — 199

FOREWORD

By Captain John M. Bailey Jr., Delta Air Lines (Retired)

In 1977, as a 700th TAS (Tactical Airlift Squadron) C-7 Caribou pilot stationed at Dobbins AFB, Georgia, I vividly recall meeting, flying with, then befriending Johnnie Jones. And even though he was a very thoughtful, intelligent, knowledgeable, and professional flight mechanic, I was unaware that he was actually in training to become a fully qualified C-7 flight mechanic with the 700th. Moreover, during our inflight conversations and in addition to becoming a fully qualified C-7 flight mechanic, I observed how he spared little time letting other pilots know of his dream to eventually become a USAF pilot as well. But, to make that happen, Johnnie knew he had to also obtain a four-year college degree. Therefore, while continuing to serve as a flight mechanic, Johnnie was already enrolled at Clark College (now Clark Atlanta University).

Furthermore, to meet both goals, he had developed a brilliant eight-year plan to serve a four-year active-duty enlistment and then use his GI Bill benefits to obtain a four-year college degree. The successful completion of his eight-year plan would put him on course to become both a USAF officer and AF pilot. The first four years of his plan required that he serve a four-year enlistment period as an aircraft mechanic. To that end, he enlisted in the Air Force, completed basic training, then completed maintenance school, and spent nearly four years at Moody AFB, Georgia, as a

T-38 and F-4 crew chief. But, in order for him to develop stick and rudder skills, my advice was for him to begin taking flying lessons at a local Atlanta-area airport as soon as possible.

Consequently, he chose to take an introductory flight lesson from a close friend—Ozzie Ross—a CFI (Certified Flight Instructor) at the Fulton County Airport, Charlie Brown Field. After that introductory flight, I knew he was hooked. And, although I was forced to leave the 700th TAS before Johnnie became an AF officer and pilot, he and I managed to maintain contact throughout the years.

Johnnie's eight-year plan ultimately led him to graduate from Clark, and complete both the USAF officer training school (OTS) and the USAF undergraduate pilot training (UPT) program at Columbus Air Force Base, Mississippi. But, while he was completing his aforementioned AF training obligations, the 700th TAS began phasing out the C-7 Caribou and replacing them with brand-new C-130 Hercules aircraft. Therefore, after completing OTS and UPT, he attended the C-130 training school in 1982. Upon his return to his squadron at Dobbins AFB, he became the unit's very first African American C-130 pilot. Then, after gaining the required flying hours to fly for the airlines, he contacted me again. But, this time to help him navigate the Delta pilot hiring process. And, even though the Delta plan was unsuccessful, he was not deterred and was ultimately hired by United Airlines, where he had a long, thirty-year airline career and retired in 2019 as a Boeing 787 Dreamliner captain. Not to be outdone by United, Captain Jones remained in the Air Force Reserves long enough to retire as a USAFR major. One of the happiest days of my life was when I was invited to attend his retirement party and witness the culmination of an extremely successful USAF/United aviation career.

Johnnie has always believed in equal rights and equal justice for all Americans. Because of his exposure to the civil rights movement while growing up in Americus, Georgia, Johnnie developed a passion for helping others by serving with his home county NAACP branch in Fayette County, Georgia. Ironically, while he was working with the Fayette County NAACP, he became aware of my work with the Atlanta NAACP and my association with the legendary Georgia icon, former executive director of the Atlanta NAACP, Ms. Jondell Johnson. All that to say, *Johnnie Jones is my hero!* He is a prime example of an African American male who had a plan, worked hard, and defied the odds to achieve his goals. And, because of his fortitude, he never quit, and because of his brilliance, Captain Johnnie Jones overcame the heavy weight of the world to get in the air and do what he loves.

Honoring my Husband, Johnnie E. Jones Jr.

Congratulations to my husband for staying the course to complete his greatest work to author his life's journey to fly airplanes, beginning as a young boy through the US Air Force and on to fly commercial airplanes. The start of his book-writing was a challenge as he gradually gained discipline and tenacity to create an outline, invest the time, and get it done. He started writing his flying and personal story during the pandemic, requiring extensive recall of factual and relevant parts of his journey. He endured previous tedious tasks and challenges that required resilience, patience, creative thinking, and extensive reading to learn successful strategies for the best outcome. His confidence is driven with self-assurance and assertiveness to succeed.

Our family and closest friends refer to Johnnie as "Edward." We are so proud of his accomplishments, commitment to succeed, and dedication to his loving family. He is a great male role model and mentor for our sons, grandsons, nieces, and nephews. He has always exhibited good qualities, with confidence and integrity, and he gives sound advice to the people of his acquaintance. Edward is a great family man, a provider, a poet, a semi-comedian, and a writer. His spiritual life and commitment to serving God are clearly demonstrated, and he knows who covered him during his air travels, domestic and abroad, over the past thirty-seven years. He often talks about his experiences growing up in Americus, Georgia, overcoming some obstacles and challenges, and moreover the ability to not fear anything. His father passed when he was almost three years of age, and he speaks about growing up without a father in his life during times when he was most needed. His dear mother was a tough lady as she provided for their family with resilience, stamina, and strength.

When we first met, it was a brief introduction, but we subsequently gained a spiritual bonding knowing we were meant to be. It was only God who led the way to unite our hearts and join us in marriage in 1995. We always had good times, some challenges, yet God led us into steadfastness to stay the course and work to make changes and to make life better for each other in spite of our differences. Our travels both domestic and abroad were most exciting, fun loving, and enjoyable. At the end of a day's work or out in the elements, we settle at home with good music, mostly jazz, gospel, and good oldies. We pretty much invented joyful noise. I am pleased with our life's journey together, and the best is yet to come.

With respect and appreciation to my love and friend,

Alice Matthews Jones

INTRODUCTION

Feeling weighed down by the troubles of the world? Going through life with the world on your shoulders can be downright stressful and overwhelming. Fortunately for most human beings, God gave us a brain, which imbues us with the capacity to figure things out. It is said that humans only use about 10 percent of their brains. This theory is the surest indication that we do not exhaust the full limits of our God-given cognitive gifts and that you should always seek knowledge (within reason). This book is about how you, too, can acquire the necessary wisdom to have peace of mind and overcome the weight of the world in more ways than one. True peace of mind comes from fully understanding how to figure things out. By the grace of God, I figured out how to fulfill my burning passion to become a jet pilot in the United States Air Force. How? When you grow up poor, Black, and live on a dead-end street, ordinarily, there is only one way to turn. Lucky for me, I figured out another way to go where I wanted. All I had to do was look up.

As I was growing up in Americus, Georgia, I would occasionally see fast-moving jets flying overhead. In fact, if I ever heard a military fighter jet streaking across my house at low altitude, I would rush outside as fast as I could to see what kind of jet it was. Of course, commercial airliners could often be seen flying over my home at thirty to forty thousand feet. That's how my ambition to become a pilot was born. Thereafter, I was filled with an undying passion to fly far away from the daily consequences of being Black, poor, and fatherless. Instinctively, I knew someday I would be flying over Americus at forty thousand feet looking down at the place where I grew up. God really is good!

Thank God for John H. Johnson and the *Ebony* magazine he started many years ago. In one edition of *Ebony* published sometime around the mid-1960s, General Daniel "Chappie" James was featured in an article. He was a big, Black, handsome four-star Air Force general who had flown F-4 Phantom II fighter jets in Vietnam. General Chappie became my main inspiration and will forever be my hero. Today, four-star General Charles Brown, who is also Black, recently managed to rise to the very top of the United States Air Force. He is also my hero because he is the Air Force chief of staff, which means he is the highest-ranking leader in the Air Force. Because of my success and theirs, I can't help but love the Air Force and appreciate the awesome opportunities it provides for my people to excel.

Fast-forward to March of 1982 when I was nearing the end of my yearlong undergraduate pilot training—the cover of this book captures the greatest achievement of my lifetime. The equipment I wore while flying the T-38 reminds me of the scripture Ephesians 6:11–18, which begins by saying, "Put on the whole armor of God, that ye may be able to stand against the wiles of the devil." Thus, you may be interested in knowing what exactly that equipment is. The green Nomex flight suit and gloves are designed to be flame-retardant in the case of a fire or crash landing. There is a parachute on my back, which is necessary in case I have to eject from the aircraft. I am also wearing a G-suit around my lower extremities with a hose that connects to the aircraft pneumatic system. The purpose of the G-suit is to keep a pilot from passing out. It inflates at high gravity loads in tight turns or pull-ups to keep the blood from draining from my head to my lower body. Lastly, my helmet is necessary to protect my head as well as provide a connection to my oxygen mask and cords so I can communicate inside and outside the aircraft. The United States Air Force deserves a lot of credit for making safety a high priority. Overall, God deserves the utmost credit for keeping me safe during hundreds of flights throughout my flying career.

Good music has been the glue that holds my life together. My love for soul-stirring soul music gives me a unique way to tell my story. As you read along, think of the sound and words of the songs that gave me inspiration and peace, and kept me going all these years. One particular song by Lionel Richie and the Commodores, entitled "Zoom," inspired me to pursue my aviation career. Many other songs of the '60s, '70s, and '80s also inspired me in one way or another. Two other very important songs for me are "Everything Must Change" by George Benson and Oleta Adams and "Dream of a Lifetime" by Marvin Gaye.

While change is constant, it is necessary to recognize that now is the only time that matters. Everything happens in the now, yet few comprehend what that really means. Our minds are programmed to focus on the past or the future. In our fixation with the past and the future, we rarely have the mental stamina to stay in the now. So, take a moment and focus on the present. When you do this, peace takes the place of those worrisome thoughts running around in our minds. That's what meditation is all about. Now, take time to reflect on your life and where God has brought you. If you want to hear someone beautifully sum up life in a song, just search for and listen to a very special song by the marvelous Marvin Gaye. As only he could do, Marvin Gaye captures the essence of my life in his song "Dream of a Lifetime."

A TRIBUTE TO OUR AFRICAN AMERICAN ANCESTORS

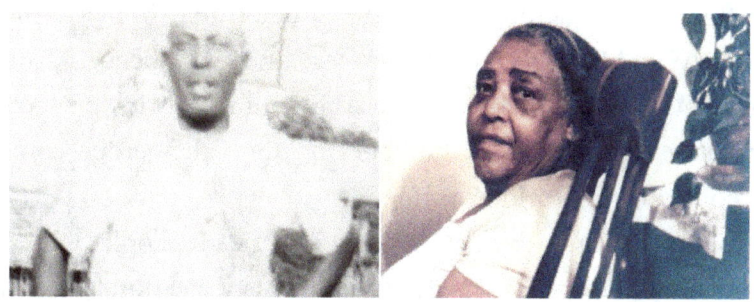

My parents were Johnnie Jones and Curley Mae Jones. They were born and raised in Middle Georgia in the early 1900s. My father grew up in the Abbeville area and was a cook on the Seaboard Railroad. Unfortunately, he died before I was three years old, so I have no recollection of him whatsoever. My mother grew up in Dooly County near Vienna. During my early years growing up in Americus, my mother worked as a domestic housekeeper in white people's houses. After my father's death in 1957, she struggled to care for my three older siblings and me. She had limited financial resources and few material possessions. And yet, somehow, we never went hungry and always had a roof over our heads, even though it leaked every darn time it rained. With this book, I pay tribute to my parents and all of my ancestors, many of whom will remain unknown due to their enslavement or the oppression they endured after slavery ended. I can only imagine what they tolerated just so I would be able to live. All I can say is thanks.

I also pay tribute to those brave African American aviators who paved the way for me to become a military pilot and a commercial airline pilot. Most notable are the Tuskegee Airmen, who trained mostly at Moton Field in Tuskegee, Alabama, in the early 1940s. President Franklin D. Roosevelt was instrumental in allowing this "experimental" program to determine if Black pilots could fly, fight, and win. The bravest of the Tuskegee Airmen, who flew P-51 Mustangs, were instrumental in protecting venerable American B-17 bombers on their dangerous combat missions during World War II.

Colored, Negro, Black, African American people who are descendants of enslaved Americans must be acknowledged for the gains they have made despite serious odds and systemic racial discrimination. Countless descendants of enslaved Americans have distinguished themselves by enduring oppressive racism in order to create a path toward equality. The African American community owes a debt of gratitude to people like Harriet Tubman, Frederick Douglass, W. E. B. Du Bois, Ida B. Wells, Booker T. Washington, Paul Robeson, Thurgood Marshall, Medgar Evers, Fannie Lou Hamer, Huey P. Newton, Malcolm X, Martin Luther King Jr., and John Lewis, whose advocacy for freedom and equality paved the way for many historic milestones for Black America. Most notably, I give credit to Dr. Martin Luther King Jr. for inspiring me to adopt the philosophy of nonviolence to advance the cause of Black people in America.

Growing Up in Americus

THE SMALL TOWN of Americus, Georgia, was a very special place to grow up, especially during the waning days of the Jim Crow era (late 1950s and early '60s). There were about seventeen thousand residents in Americus during my childhood days. Even though Black people constituted a slim majority of the population, white people owned and firmly controlled virtually everything. Other than owning a funeral home, a nightclub, car repair business, or a small neighborhood store, Black people had to rely on working for white people in order to earn a living in Americus. Regardless of their status or income level, "Negroes" or "Colored people," as we were called back then, were expected to be subservient and show reverence to white folks. White people thought nothing of cutting in front of Black people in a line at the bank or elsewhere, or calling a Black person the "N-word" whenever they desired with no consequences whatsoever. The overall goal was to instill fear into Black people, and to a large extent, it worked very well. The white police routinely treated us with utter disrespect and were quick to beat a disrespectful Black person at will if they wanted to.

I recall when the first two Black police officers were hired. For some reason, they were called Spic and Span. At first, we Black folks were happy that we finally had someone who looked like us to protect and serve us. Unfortunately, they couldn't arrest white people and were likely to be more brutal to Black people in order to prove to their white supervisors they were worthy of being cops. There was little anyone could do about the way Black people were treated until after the civil rights movement began to change attitudes.

I do recall efforts to boost our self-esteem despite the oppressive conditions. Early in my school days, Wednesday was dress-up day and boys had to wear a nice shirt and tie along with dress pants and shoes. I suppose the girls had to dress up as well. Overall, Black folks in Americus had much more dignity then, despite being oppressed on a daily basis.

The separate and unequal conditions of that time period left many Black people in and around Americus working menial jobs. Most Black people were less wealthy, less educated, and less healthy than their white townsfolk, and were often depressed, but somehow most of us remained determined to do whatever it took to challenge racism. Nonetheless, those "Negroes" who dared to protest segregation and advocate for equal rights were often arrested and jailed. During the summer of 1963, when I was nine years old, a group of teenage "Negro" girls was arrested and jailed in an old, dilapidated Civil War stockade in Leesburg,

Georgia. For a while, no one knew where they were, as many of them were caged for months in a large cell without access to adequate drinking water, food, or toilet facilities. Some of these "Leesburg Stockade Girls" were people I knew, and they endured this ordeal with such dignity that few knew what really happened to them.

A group of teenage "Negro" boys suffered a similar experience of being arrested and jailed for protesting. The boys were loaded onto a tractor-trailer truck and shipped off to jail in surrounding counties or cities like Dawson. Sammy Mahone was a brave civil rights activist and one of those teenage boys who were jailed. He is now determined to ensure that the story of these brave "Negro" teenagers is preserved for future generations to learn about the civil rights movement in Americus and in the rest of Sumter County.

Americus is the county seat of Sumter County, and my family settled there in the late '40s before I was born. I grew up on Beale Street, a name synonymous with the blues, and we definitely had our share of blues. It was a dusty red dirt road for most of my time in Americus until two resilient Black people who owned a local grocery store began to challenge the status quo. Ms. Bessie Mays and her brother, Mr. Hope Merritt, decided to ask for our street to be paved. Although Black people paid taxes like white folks, the bulk of our tax dollars was going into the maintenance or improvement of white neighborhoods. Interestingly, former President Jimmy Carter grew up and lived in Plains, Georgia, which is just ten miles away from Americus, but I never got to see or meet him.

I grew up as the youngest of six children. Currently, I have my two sisters, Denise and Elizabeth, and my one and only older brother, Kirby. My brother Kirby's last name is Ragins, and his dad was Charlie Ragin. Somehow, Kirby's last name became Ragins when he joined the Air Force. His father's marriage to our mother ended around the time she moved from Orlando, Florida, to Americus, where she met and married my dad in 1950. Our next older sister was Linda, who is now deceased. Linda lived with us briefly and lived nearby for most of her life. We never got to live with our sister Virginia, who is also now deceased, because she was much older and had gotten married and started her own family by the time my mother moved to Americus. Virginia's husband, Joseph Floyd Sr., was an outstanding career Army man and Korean War veteran who always encouraged me, especially when he found out about my military aspirations. Joseph Floyd Sr. had such a strong stature and presence that I couldn't help being inspired by his wise counsel and much-welcomed encouragement. To me, he could have been an Army general because he looked the part and had so much wisdom and pride in himself.

My childhood home in Americus, Georgia

My family lived in what could be described as a fairly primitive house, even by the standards of the time. Our house was little more than a roof over our heads. Whenever it rained, we scrambled to move furniture and put out pots to catch the rainwater. Our home had no indoor plumbing, and the outhouse was the only toilet besides the pot we used in the house. We had to get water from the faucet at the front porch, heat the water on the gas stove, and use a round metal tub for bathing. For heat during the icy cold winters, all we had was kerosene heaters and a fireplace. There were many days we had to chop wood for the fireplace or use coal, if we could afford it. Yet and still, if it weren't for the quilts and blankets that our mother made or acquired, we would have frozen to death. We had fans for air conditioning during the sweltering hot Georgia summers. Washing clothes was often done with a rubboard in a tin tub and dried on the outdoor clothesline. Nevertheless, it was my home for over seventeen long years, and a place I shall never forget.

My father, Johnnie Sr., was a cook in the caboose on the Seaboard Railroad trains. My mother, Curley Mae, worked hard as a domestic housekeeper in white people's houses. By the way, the money she earned was barely enough to survive.

I was born in 1954, the same year as the historic Supreme Court decision known as *Brown v. Board of Education*. On paper, this law struck down the old separate-but-equal doctrine that legally kept Black people from going to the better-funded white schools. It would take another sixteen years before the law took full effect when mandatory school integration began in 1970, which was my junior year in high school.

While my mother was working during the days before I began elementary school, my uncle Robert Jones (whom I fondly called Uncle Bo) or a family friend known as Mrs. Jeanette Whitehead cared for me during the day. Uncle Bo, my dad's brother, was a man of few words who suffered from periodic violent epileptic seizures. Somewhere around 1950, my dad had brought him from

Abbeville, Georgia, to live with us on Beale Street. I remember the first time I saw him have an epileptic fit. He fell out and his body started violently shaking as he foamed at the mouth. Someone instinctively knew to put rag or something in his mouth to keep him from biting his tongue. I understand that he was unable to work a real job due to his dreadful disability.

In July 1957, just before I turned three years of age, my fifty-four-year-old father suddenly died from a heart attack while on a trip with the Seaboard Railroad in Stewart County. Unfortunately, I have no recollection of him. At some point in my childhood, I discovered that my father had an older daughter named Curtis Banks who resided in Philadelphia. Apparently, she had two sons named Johnnie Banks and Alvin Banks. Writing letters to people far away was always exciting to me. Curtis and I would write letters to each other, but I never had the chance to see or talk to her. This would be the first of many interesting connections with the city of Philadelphia.

After my dad's death, my mother eventually began receiving benefit checks from the Railroad Retirement Board survivor benefits for Elizabeth, Denise, and me. Regrettably, as each of us turned eighteen, the survivor benefit check was reduced. I do vaguely recall Sunday visits to my father's gravesite, where I once placed a bright-red caboose from a trainset I had gotten for Christmas. I am told I am just like my dad, but it is disheartening not to remember what his voice sounded like, or what his favorite pastimes were. Nevertheless, I guess ole Uncle Bo tried to fill in for my dad, but he was in for a treat. He would soon learn that I could be difficult to handle. My older brother Kirby and I shared a room with Uncle Bo. Usually, Uncle Bo would get up early and go across the street to the local store, where he did odd jobs when not sitting on the store's porch.

My mother was someone I learned many life lessons from just by watching her go about her daily life. Faced with having to raise four younger children all by herself in the latter part of the '50s and all through the '60s, she had to be a praying woman. The rent on our little house was twenty dollars a month, and she could barely afford it. She was constantly in debt to finance companies that preyed on Black people back then. I recall her paying upward of 25 percent interest on a loan, and it seemed she would never be able to pay it off. She probably earned twenty dollars a week from the low-paying domestic housekeeper jobs she had. Nevertheless, she was absolutely masterful at caring and providing for her children. I watched her add bread to ground beef or milk to eggs to stretch the portions so we could all have enough to eat. Her fried chicken was the best ever, and everything she cooked was good.

On her domestic housekeeping jobs, I can imagine she had to put on a happy face to endure the racism that came with that job. Perhaps that's why I would anxiously await her coming home during the days of my youth. She wore a white uniform dress to work, and I distinctly remember how I would play in the front yard and spot her coming down Beale Street with her pocketbook on her arm. As she got closer, I would run as fast as I could to greet her with open arms. Some people are raised knowing both parents and most or all of their grandparents, but it never occurred to me back then that she was the one and only parent I had to count on. In contrast, our closest next door neighbors and lifelong family friends Ozie and Jesse Pope were raised by their grandparents. Jesse and I had some fun times especially when he allowed me to help him deliver Americus Times Recorder newspapers on his paper route.

There is a scene at the end of the movie *The Help* where Viola Davis's character is fired and she walks home with her pocketbook on her arm. As I sat in a theater watching this scene play out, vivid memories of my mother came rushing back to me, and all of a sudden, I burst into tears. All I could think about as I watched the movie was all of the racism, misery, and pain my mother had to deal with on a daily basis all her life, like the character in the movie. Furthermore, I could imagine that the daily toll of racism and inequality probably conspired to shorten my dad's life too. That's why I have very little tolerance for racism today. Regrettably, racism is still a persistent barrier for Black people.

As I mentioned before, there were days before I started going to school when Uncle Bo would be my caretaker while my mother worked and my older siblings were in school. I remember one day when I was around four years old, I was being mischievous by burning kerosene in a coffee can in the backyard when Uncle Bo caught me. He said, "What you doin', boy?" I panicked and kicked the can over, spewing fire onto the grass. Being the brave man he was, Uncle Bo saved the day by stomping out the fire while I ran off. Fortunately for me, I played with fire and didn't get burned thanks to Uncle Bo. Somewhere along the way, Uncle Bo found a new place to live in a group home, and we rarely ever saw him. Regrettably, we never thought to ask him about our father's family, so there's very little known about that side of the family. It appears my father was born in Pulaski County, Georgia, and raised in the town of Abbeville in Wilcox County.

In addition to that, Uncle Bo taught me how to tie my shoes, and I will always be grateful for that too. Most notably, Uncle Bo was the go-to guy whenever someone saw a snake. He would fearlessly kill any snake that threatened our community.

Around 1959, I started kindergarten at what was once the Americus Colored Hospital. I recall learning my ABCs and my numbers while having to take naps in the afternoon. Interestingly, the same place where I went to kindergarten is being restored to serve as a civil rights history center. Americus civil rights activist Sammy Mahone deserves commendation for leading the effort to restore that historic building.

One of my favorite TV shows during that time was *No Time for Sergeants*, starring Andy Griffith. The show was a comedy about the adventures of airmen in the Air Force. That was my first introduction to life in the military. Like in the show, when I became an airman years later, it was the fun times I remember the most. Other activities I enjoyed with family members were watching the made-for-TV movie *A Raisin in the Sun*, starring Sidney Poitier. For those who may have never heard of Sidney Poitier, he was as famous as Denzel Washington is today. It would be years before I fully understood the multiple messages in this 1961 movie with an all-Black cast. The rare opportunity to see people who look like you in movies or on television was the ultimate inspiration for Black people in the '60s.

The first movie I went to see in the local theater was *Thunder Road*, starring Robert Mitchum. It was about a white guy transporting moonshine liquor, which was an illegal activity that many people, Black and white, engaged in back in the day. At the time, I didn't understand why my family and I had to pay at the rear of the movie theater and proceed upstairs to the "Colored" section. This was one of the first of many encounters I had with racial segregation that really made no sense at all. Nevertheless, it made sense to white people, who didn't want us anywhere near them.

School Days and Childhood Memories

AS I BEGAN my elementary school education in the fall of 1960, my brother Kirby took me to school to introduce me to my first-grade teacher. John Fitzgerald Kennedy was the president at that time. Black people thought highly of President Kennedy because he gave us hope that someday we "Negroes" would be able to live as first-class citizens. On the other hand, I felt a deep discomfort with having to mindlessly recite the Pledge of Allegiance in school. "With liberty and justice for all" is the disturbing phrase that left me confused, because I knew without a doubt that my Black people were not totally free like white folks.

I loved watching TV but was bothered by the lack of quality Black shows. This was a time when there were no Black people in commercials at all. None! In later years, I would watch every episode of military shows on TV, such as *Combat*, and especially the thrilling flying show *Twelve O'Clock High*. This World War II weekly television show was about Army Air Corp aircrews flying B-17 bombers out of England to missions over Germany. It was through these shows and movies about World War II that I fell in love with the military and with flying. Playing with little green army men was another one of my favorite pastimes.

My first-grade photo

Almost every night, I would stay up until the TV signed off at midnight so I could watch the video showing an Air Force jet flying high in the sky while a white man eloquently recited the poem "High Flight" by John Gillespie Magee Jr. As I watched that jet soar through the skies and listened to those magical words, I could see myself in that jet. Couple that experience with the days when a fast-moving military jet would streak across the sky above our house, and I was hooked on the idea of flying for a living.

In school, there were times when I would make paper airplanes and sail them across the classroom when my teachers weren't looking. There was no end to my imagination and desire to fly jets. But how could a poor Black kid from Americus become a jet pilot in the Air Force? Put another way, how could I overcome the weight of the world and get in the air and do what I love?

Thanks to my mother, I developed an intense interest at an early age in reading books she bought for me. That led me to visit the library as often as I could. In the school library I found a green book entitled *Jet Pilot*. I checked it out and read it cover to cover. That book about a white guy going through undergraduate pilot training in the Air Force and subsequently training as an F-100 Super Sabre jet pilot was oh so inspiring. Thereafter, I read the sequel, *Jet Pilot Overseas*, and was even more inspired. As if I was along for the adventure, these books would prepare me for what was to come years later. While I didn't see or read about one Black pilot anywhere in those books, I was undeterred by the obvious burden of racism that kept many Black men and women on the outside looking in. For what it was worth, I knew absolutely nothing about the Black military servicemen called the Tuskegee Airmen and their brave service during World War II. I now understand the Tuskegee Airmen "experiment" was intentionally kept secret, or rarely discussed or publicized, until much later in my life.

As my classmates and I ventured through the '60s going to school and doing homework, I became quite adventurous, as boys are supposed to be. I was so motivated by my newfound passion that I diligently progressed through each grade with passing scores. Naturally, I spent a lot of time climbing trees in my youth, because I always enjoyed being up high in the sky. In fact, there were two tall pecan trees in our backyard that I would climb every chance I got. My childhood friend Russell and I would get together most days after school or during the summers. We dug tunnels in the backyard and rode stick horses around the neighborhood. Once I climbed one of the pecan trees in our backyard with my walkie-talkie to see if I could talk to Russell, who lived about half a mile away from my house. We were shouting so loud we probably could have heard each other without those cheap-ass walkie-talkies. We still laugh about that today.

But it was not all fun and games during my childhood. There were those days when my mother would make me help her in the garden, tending to collard greens, corn, cane stalks, peas, and other crops. Most notably, I remember going to the cotton fields in the summertime with many of my neighbors. Back then, wealthy white landowners relied heavily on the cheap labor provided by poor "Negroes" who picked tons of cotton in the hot summers. Early in the mornings, a big truck would ride through our neighborhood gathering up those "Negroes" who wanted to make some money, mostly chump change. We would be out in the cotton fields all day long just to make a few cents per pound of cotton picked. They learned quickly that I was no good at picking cotton, so they made my sister Denise and me ride the water wagon to keep everybody hydrated. Being in the cotton fields was as close to the experience of being enslaved as I could imagine. That experience served as motivation for me to dream big dreams and aim high, because doing manual labor or getting my hands dirty was not something I was interested in as a career.

In the early '60s, Black folks loved President Kennedy because we were hopeful he would support getting rid of the Jim Crow laws that had held us back for so long. Sadly, I remember that dark day on November 22, 1963, when President Kennedy was assassinated in Dallas, Texas. I was in my third-grade class when the announcement came over the loudspeaker. Fortunately for us

Black folks, Lyndon B. Johnson became president and ultimately passed critical civil rights legislation that helped Black people move a little closer to real freedom and equality.

When Dr. Martin Luther King Jr. and the civil rights movement began to agitate and advocate for freedom, equality, and justice, we Black folks in Americus did our part too. I recall being in a massive protest march somewhere around 1963 or 1964 when I was about nine years old. The march through downtown Americus was very organized, with us walking two by two. As we turned the corner to march down the main street to the courthouse, there was a long line of Black faces in either direction as far as I could see. This was the first time I realized the population of my little hometown was mostly Black and we weren't going to let anybody turn us around. There's an old Sam Cooke song entitled "A Change Is Gonna Come" that reminds me of that day and time.

Nevertheless, change was slow to come. One day while playing in my front yard, I witnessed a white police officer in his patrol car riding down Beale Street alongside a Black man who was walking home. After the officer inquired about the contents of a bag the Black man had in his hand, the Black man bolted and ran in between two houses. The police officer got out of his car and fired a shot at the fleeing Black man. Fortunately, the bullet missed him, and he got away. This was when I realized Black lives really didn't matter to most white people back then, and sometimes it seems it doesn't matter much today.

Somehow, I always remained hopeful things would someday change for the better. Brave leaders like the Rev. Robert Freeman brought in freedom fighters like Dr. King and John Lewis to motivate us. One of my favorite activities was to attend mass meetings at Rev. Freeman's church, Bethesda Missionary Baptist Church, with friends like Phil Merritt and Russell Moye. We were much too young to know the severity of the civil rights movement, but I have nothing but admiration for civil rights leaders who helped change things for the better.

In the white neighborhood in Americus near my home, there was a beautiful taxpayer-funded public swimming pool. I used to ride my bicycle through that area and sometimes got chased out of the neighborhood or called bad names. Unfortunately, Jim Crow laws strictly prevented us "Colored" folks from swimming in that public pool. So, naturally, we found the nearby Muckalee Creek to be the next best place to cool off during the long, hot summers. Getting to Muckalee Creek required following a trail through the backwoods and railroad tracks near the end of Beale Street, including a dangerous walk across an elevated train trestle.

One hot summer day while I was swimming in the creek along with some other neighborhood kids, I ventured into the deep part of the creek and began to drown. My life flashed before me. I can still see the nasty brown water I was swallowing as I gasped for air. All of a sudden, a strong, God-like hand pulled me out and somehow revived me. At that very moment, I could have been dead and gone, but it seems God had much more for me to do. As a result of that experience, I somehow knew subconsciously from then on that no one dies until God is ready for them to die. Although I didn't realize it, this was my first indication that everything that happens has to happen. I managed to repress the memory of this near-fatal event until years later when I went to visit Alvin Bowen in Los Angeles in 1974. Alvin, who is six years older than I am, became my guardian angel that day. I am forever indebted to my childhood neighbor and lifelong friend for saving my life that day. He and his late brother Junior Bowens (or "Big Dude") were just like two more big brothers to me in addition to my big brother Kirby.

In this book, I wish to pay a special tribute to the memory of William Bowens Jr. He was someone who was so jovial and fun to be around that I never, ever contemplated a day when he would not be alive. I relished being in his presence whenever I could because I knew I would learn something, or he would make me laugh out loud. I jokingly said to him one day that he should have been a preacher. Junior wasted no time responding when he said, "I don't play with God!" Nevertheless, on the day of his funeral, the hearse that carried his body to the burial ground at Andersonville National Cemetery near ran into the back of the preacher's car. We laughed for a while because everybody who knew him knew that "Dude" had to have something to do with that wreck.

At my father's gravesite in Americus

One of the most soothing things that provided a great deal of peace of mind and enjoyment for Black folks then, as now, was good ole soul and soul-stirring gospel music. There were memorable classic songs of that day and time such as "Georgia on My Mind" by Ray Charles, which is a song that never gets old. To this day, I always love to hear Ray sing that song because there's something very special about the state of Georgia and the way he sings that song. Perhaps that's the reason I have never had a real desire to live anywhere other than Georgia. Georgia is "the land where my fathers died" as they say in the song "My Country 'Tis of Thee."

In the fifth grade at Eastview Elementary School, my classroom was not far from my father's gravesite in Eastview Cemetery. Back then, schools had lots of windows, which I believe somehow made a difference in learning. I always appreciated seeing the natural daylight coming through the windows which brightened my day. There were many days when I would gaze out the classroom window looking toward the cemetery and experience a gut-wrenching emptiness that no one could ever understand, much less experience. For decades, I have wondered to myself what his voice sounded like, what kind of food he liked to eat, what kind of music he liked to hear, or what he liked to do for fun. I couldn't help but envy my friends who had a father around. All I could do was try to find strong male role models to emulate as I struggled to live without my dad. Mere words cannot convey the anguish of a young Black boy who does not have the benefit of knowing his father or having his father around. It's strange when all a boy or man has to remember his father by is his concrete gravesite and a faded headstone. Deep down inside it hurt like pure hell not to have a father in my life, while so many of my friends did. I grieved silently for years as I sought to make sense of it and to find some way to make him proud.

As my childhood years went by, I began to feel the weight of the world on my shoulders. In the earlier years, my mother took us to Friendship Baptist Church on the other side of town on Cotton Avenue. I used to wonder why we didn't go to the church near our home, but I realized my mother wanted to attend the church where her sister, Aunt Mariah Reeves, attended. While I gained an appreciation for religion and Christianity over time, I always wanted to gain a deeper understanding of the mysterious aspects of believing in God and the real purpose of the Bible. I also developed an intense desire to understand human behavior and was very curious about the unknown mysteries of religion. My pastor at that time, the Rev. Daniel Thomas, was the best preacher I have ever heard, because he could sing as well as he could preach. At the end of most of his soul-stirring sermons, at least one old lady would be shouting and praising God. One of the songs I used to love to hear him sing was "In That Land Where I'm Bound."

It is noteworthy that many gospel songs heard in the Black church seem to glorify death, perhaps to get us to endure the pains of being Black in America. Somewhere around the age of five, I recall getting baptized and the Rev. Thomas saying, "Boy, you look like you're going to be a preacher." Back then, I reckon, he couldn't even imagine saying, "Boy, you look like you're going to be a pilot," because systemic racial discrimination limited a Black man's career choices mostly to being a preacher or a teacher or entrepreneur if he wanted to earn a decent living. That's one of the ways the damaging legacy of slavery and racism had adversely affected our entire race.

Strangely, it would take songs from Earth, Wind & Fire and Marvin Gaye to stimulate my interest in religion years later. Over time, my mother went from taking us to church to sending us to church. She struggled off and on with paying bills, despair, diabetes, and other life challenges for years. The gospel song entitled "Nobody Knows the Trouble I've Seen" by Paul Robeson comes to mind when I think of my mother and the troubles she saw during her life.

Ever since I could remember, my mother had a nasty sore on one of her ankles that would not heal no matter what she did. She would be on her feet working all day for white folks and then come home and prepare a meal for her children. We would learn later she had diabetes, but she had no medical insurance and couldn't afford to go to a doctor. By God's grace she was able to nurse that wound and kept on going like the Energizer bunny.

On one occasion, she took me to work with her at the Sheffields', a wealthy white family that lived on the north side of Americus in a very nice house. I even played with the Sheffield boys, and quite surprisingly, they were nice to me. The Sheffields owned a hardware store in Americus and sold a variety of things, including toys. That was probably why I would get almost every toy I wanted for Christmas in my early years.

The only other close interaction I had ever had with white people before the Sheffield boys was when our next-door neighbor, also a domestic worker, would bring a little white boy home with her. Ms. Hicks would let this white fellow and me play together since we were about the same age. I don't remember his name, but it would be many years before I would have any other interactions with white folks.

Several events shaped my life from the sixth to the tenth grade, which spanned from 1966 through 1970. While in the sixth grade, a peculiar incident occurred in our home that taught me how to handle physical pain. Because our home had no inside running water, we had an old metal pot that we used to get tap water from the faucet at the front porch. We could then carry it into the house to be heated on the kitchen stove. That pot had a broken handle with a screw on one side that required the use of a rag to safely carry it. One time when my sister was taking her bath water to the metal tub we used for bathing, I passed her right as she accidentally dropped that boiling-hot pot of water.

As the hot water splashed up onto my right thigh, it felt like I was on fire, so I instinctively stopped, dropped, and rolled as if I was trying to put it out the fire burning my leg. My mother immediately administered first aid and used clever home medical remedies to treat the second-degree burns and painful blisters that rose up on my upper thigh. There was no thought of going to the hospital or to see a doctor, as we had no medical insurance or money for medical care. Although I enjoyed the two-mile walk across town to the segregated Staley High School, walking to school with those blisters was memorable. Most of all, I knew my sister meant me absolutely no harm, and she and I remain very close to this day. In fact, all of my living siblings remain close mainly because of the various shared lifelong experiences we encountered and cherish. Thank God for the family love we share.

By a curious twist of circumstances, the white high school that was very close to my home attracted the attention of a few Black students who decided to give it a try even though segregation was still partially in force. I, too, could have volunteered to go to the previously all-white Americus High School, which was less than a mile from my house, but I didn't know if I could tolerate the racism and hate I was sure to face. At Staley, we would be issued used textbooks just like we had in elementary school. Our old textbooks had been used by the white students first and then handed down to us "Negroes." Much to our benefit, a strict disciplinarian and teacher named Mr. Clyde McGrady embraced my class. Mr. McGrady would eventually become a teacher who would stay with my class year after year all the way through high school. Also, he became the best teacher I've ever had because you could tell he cared about us. Of course, we were paddled when we misbehaved, and these disciplinary measures were very effective at making sure we respected our teachers. Other memorable teachers who showed love for my classmates and me were Ms. Effie Daniels, Mr. Otis

Carter, Ms. Eloise Douglas, Ms. Teresa Mansfield, Ms. Eddie Rhea Walker, and Mr. John King, to name a few.

When I was out of school, I spent many days in my backyard just sitting and thinking about life or how to figure things out. Quite frankly, who knows what would have happened to me if it weren't for my ability to rationalize and to nurture an insatiably strong ambition to become an Air Force pilot. Many Saturday mornings were spent thinking for hours and hours as I lay in the top bunk in the bedroom my brother Kirby and I shared. I would daydream for hours about the life I wanted and try to figure out how to help my mother have a better life.

There are some very important things in life that I dreamed about having one day. One of my greatest hopes of all was to have a loving, dedicated future wife and four wonderful children, two boys and two girls. I hoped my future wife would be compatible, intelligent, humble, and able to put up with me through any and everything. The unforgettable song entitled "Stay in My Corner" by the Dells captured the essence of what kind of soulmate relationship I desperately wanted someday. Overall, the two things I wanted most in life were to be an Air Force pilot and to have the ideal woman and wife to share my life with. Every good man needs a dedicated female companion who knows how to love him, appreciate him, and support him through thick and thin.

As I discovered, neither becoming a pilot nor finding a good wife would be easy, probably because I didn't have enough sense to pray for what I wanted back then. At that time, it seemed my prayers to a faraway God up in heaven probably wouldn't get through anyhow. Fortunately, I would later learn that prayer is essentially an appeal to the God that is within me. In adulthood, I even wrote a poem with a line that says, "When ye pray, who hears what you say? It's the God in you who hears what you pray." It was also extremely important for me to learn to be patient. More specifically, I had to learn delayed gratification, which would become one of the best life lessons ever. I had to learn how to plan ahead, stay laser-focused, and be very patient.

Nothing worthwhile has ever come to me easily. As far as becoming a jet pilot, I had to totally rely on myself for motivation because there wasn't a pilot in my community to talk to or emulate. Besides that, no one really believed in my dream of becoming a pilot but me.

In 1967, my brother Kirby got a draft notice and cleverly joined the Air Force to avoid the possibility of having to be a foot soldier getting shot at in Vietnam. Prior to that, several other older childhood friends had joined the military. "Greetings (This Is Uncle Sam)" by the Monitors was a popular song that came out in 1966, around the time Charles Brooks, Willie Dennis Harvey, and William "Junior" Bowens had either joined the Army or were drafted. Willie C. "Bruh" Merritt and his brother James Merritt joined the Air Force. My savior from Muckalee Creek, Alvin Bowens, joined the Air Force in 1966 too. These guys inspired me and showed me how military service was the perfect avenue to escape the drudgery of Americus. It is also very ironic that five Black boys from Beale Street chose to join the United States Air Force, which gave all of us a terrific foundation in life.

Me at fourteen at home on Beale Street

Around the tender age of twelve, I also had another professional interest—to be a long-haul truck driver. I loved big trucks and still do. Other than a trip to Orlando, Florida, I had never been outside of Georgia, so I begged my mother to let me ride with a truck driver named Jerry Huff back in 1967. My trip all the way to Anna, Illinois, was my fondest and most memorable. Americus was a manufacturing hub for mobile homes and Jerry had to take a huge load of mobile home parts on a blue flatbed tandem-wheel Chevy truck to a company that assembled mobile homes.

We left Americus after sundown, and he drove all night through Alabama, Mississippi, and Kentucky to arrive in Illinois the next morning. Most notably, I recall us going down a road near Columbus, Mississippi, where I saw a yellow road sign that read, LOW-FLYING AIRCRAFT. Little did I know that years later, I would be in one of those low-flying aircraft training to be an Air Force pilot. How ironic is that?

On another trip down to Lake City, Florida, to pick up chemicals for what we called the acid plant in Americus that made fertilizer, Jerry had me switch places with him in the driver's seat while rolling down the interstate highway known as I-75. And there I was sitting behind the big wheel of a tractor-trailer truck at the tender age of fourteen. One of the things I learned about eighteen-wheelers was the inability to tell where the end of the trailer is because there is no depth perception when looking into the rearview mirror. That's why I try to give trucks plenty of room to change lanes, or I flash my headlights to let them know it's okay to pull in front of me when I am driving. To this day, I have the utmost respect and admiration for truck drivers. Thanks to Jerry, I got to drive a big truck for a few miles down I-75. Incidentally, Jerry Huff is the father of my nephew Marcus Huff, who followed his dad into trucking as well.

In 1969, Kirby came home on military leave and took me to see the Air Force Thunderbirds flight demonstration team perform at Robins Air Force Base in Warner Robins, Georgia. I got the chance to see numerous Air Force jets on display that I had only read about, and the real thrill was seeing the Thunderbirds flying the lightning-fast F-4 Phantom jets. The highlight of the air show was seeing the solo Thunderbird pilot fly at six hundred miles per hour past the crowd, so low and so fast the roaring of the engines was several seconds behind the aircraft. What a magnificent treat! Thanks, Kirby! You're the best brother ever!

My sister Elizabeth had three classmates who had a profound impact on me without them knowing it. Whenever Gloria Jordan, Betty Shelton, or Cora Butts saw me at school, they would call me "pilot." While this was an affectionate way of acknowledging my ambition, being called "pilot" while I was just a high school student encouraged me to become one. This is why I try to do the same for any ambitious young person.

The year 1968 proved to be an extraordinarily turbulent time for the United States of America. With strong ambitions of being in the military, I did become conflicted due to the troubling details about the contentious civil rights struggle, multiple assassinations, big-city riots, and the bloody Vietnam war with weekly American casualties averaging around five hundred dead soldiers a week. Additionally, hundreds of American military aircraft were being shot down each year in Vietnam. On the home front, the Black Panthers emerged as an inspiration to millions of Black people, including me. James Brown's hit record "Say It Loud—I'm Black and I'm Proud" provided immense inspiration as well. The assassination of Dr. Martin Luther King Jr. proved to be a major tragedy that had a tremendous impact on me as well as my race. It's no wonder my people often sought to escape our misery by drinking alcohol, using drugs, or partying.

Our side of town was called the Seaboard Side because of the train tracks that bordered our neighborhood belonging to the Seaboard Coast Line Railroad. At the end of Beale Street, we had a juke joint named the Rocket 88, which may as well have been called the Rockin' 88. For some strange reason, the popular nightclub on the other side of town was called the Astro, which also had some semblance of traveling to outer space. Maybe those names came from oppressed Black folks wanting to be out of this world.

For most of my high school years I was a loner; few people wanted to associate with me because I was poor and from the so-called "bad side" of town. Nevertheless, some of the most decent people lived near me, but it was hard to escape the stigma of being from Beale Street. Some classmates made fun of me because I was left-handed, flat-headed, or for any other thing they could find to tease me about. Yet, thanks to my tenacious mother, I had dignity in the midst of despair. Yes, a few guys from the other side of town bullied me. Also, I did get into a few fights with guys who didn't like me for one reason or another. Overall, I tried to practice non-violence as Dr. King urged us to do. On one occasion, I read a book to learn how to box so I could teach a bully to respect me. This was just one of many times I satisfied my thirst for knowledge by reading a book about something that would benefit me. Ultimately, I adopted a logical philosophy about fighting. I decided I would refuse to fight anyone, but would readily defend myself. At times it was hard not having a real friend like Russell. He was the first true friend I ever had in life, and after he moved away to Newark, I couldn't find another really close friend in Americus.

Before I got my driver's license, I would walk all the way across town to the teenage dance at the Masonic Lodge on Friday or Saturday nights. Yes, there were many times when my self-esteem was low, but I was always able to handle the loneliness. In fact, I enjoyed being by myself because it allowed me time to think about my future. Some of my peers who didn't care much for me tried to label me with unwanted, ugly nicknames. In order to avoid getting stuck with a nickname I didn't care for, I decided to call myself JET JONES and even had a football jersey made with that name on the back. I realized years later that my self-appointed nickname, JET JONES, would subconsciously motivate me to fulfill my greatest ambition.

In bold defiance of the pervasive but stupid superstitions that had routinely instilled baseless fear in my life, I also put the number thirteen on that jersey. Initially, I told myself I had adopted the name JET JONES because I wanted to play high school football and be a fast-running back. The only problem with that idea was I wasn't that fast and was cut from the football team early on. I also got cut from the basketball team. It didn't help that the Black and white schools finally merged in 1970, so they had twice as many football players at the integrated Americus High School that year.

My friend Willie Kent Johnson and I as high school seniors

In high school, I developed a passion for writing, but my English teachers would mark up my papers with red ink so badly that I became discouraged. Many years would pass before I returned to writing, which I consider my second passion. Because of my love for aviation, I remember getting a good grade for a paper I wrote about the principles of flight. My paper included an explanation of the four forces that act on an aircraft: lift, weight, thrust, and drag.

My classmate Willie Kent Johnson, who came down from Philadelphia Pennsylvania to finish high school, was a good friend too. He was the second connection to Philadelphia I had. Willie and

I became good friends and had some good clean fun during our senior year in high school. Mike Anthony was another good Beale Street friend who was younger than me. I tried my best to keep him encouraged. Mike and I would hang out together and even dated two girls who were sisters. Some of my other peers got into underage drinking and smoking marijuana, and these were some of the real reasons I had few friends while growing up in Americus. I had a deep opposition to doing anything that would jeopardize my freedom or my potential career as a pilot.

Besides that, music provided me with everything I needed to deal with the weight of the world at that time. While some of my peers would crave "getting high" by doing illegal drugs or drinking alcohol, I would be satisfied with listening to some good ole soothing soul music or jazz. I reasoned that drugs and alcohol are essentially traps set out for Black people, and far too often our people take the bait and suffer the consequences. Nevertheless, all we have ever had to do is use the brains God gave us to figure things out. Besides that, nothing was going to keep me from becoming an Air Force pilot.

These were intense times for Black people, and racial strife was an ever-present threat. As I stated before, I also give Dr. Martin Luther King Jr. credit for getting me to internalize the logic and power of nonviolence, because at one time violence seemed to be the only answer to the challenges Black people faced. A very inspirational movie entitled *Shaft* and two very influential albums came out in 1971. Isaac Hayes's soundtrack album *Shaft* emboldened every Black male, and Marvin Gaye's album *What's Going On* became the most motivating music of a lifetime. The title song was about Marvin's brother returning from a tour of duty in Vietnam and asking, "What's going on?" To this day Black people are still asking the same question.

Around this time, I began exploring routes I needed to take to become an Air Force pilot. For a high school graduate, there were three main ways to become an Air Force pilot. You could apply to the Air Force Academy, try to get an Air Force ROTC scholarship, or get a degree from a four-year college and apply for Officer Training School (OTS). First, I submitted a formal request to my congressional representatives to be nominated to the Air Force Academy. To my dismay, I was selected as a ninth alternate, which meant eight other people had to decline their academy appointment before I would get a shot at going to the Air Force Academy. Thereafter, I applied for an Air Force ROTC scholarship but was turned down when I didn't obtain a passing score on the Air Force Officer Qualifying Test (AFOQT).

Furthermore, I had to take a physical exam at Robins AFB around 1971 and a racist white Air Force doctor indicated on my record that I had a disqualifying heart murmur. His words never even entered my consciousness because deep down I knew somehow that his diagnosis had absolutely no validity to it. Feeling the heavy weight of disappointment at being denied an appointment to the Air Force Academy, and then being turned down for the scholarship, I felt like my chances of becoming an Air Force officer were becoming dim.

The final way to become an Air Force pilot was to obtain a four-year college degree and successfully complete Air Force Officer Training School. Getting an appointment to the Air Force Academy, which was a free way to get a college education in exchange for military service, was no longer an option. Securing a four-year Air Force ROTC scholarship to attend a school like Georgia Tech or Tuskegee Institute, which I had planned to do, was out of reach when I graduated from high school. Thus, I was left with my one and only final option. I could go to college at my own expense or seek scholarships elsewhere. Unfortunately, my grades were not that spectacular and the competition for scholarship money was steep. Most notably, when I graduated from high school in 1972, my mother would no longer get a regular survivor benefit check from the Railroad Retirement Board. And just like that, the weight of the world got a little bit heavier. I needed to look far into the future to determine exactly where I needed to be eight years later. This was when I took the time to develop a detailed eight-year plan to obtain a college degree and get into Air Force pilot training before the twenty-seven-and-a-half age limit. My honorable enlisted Air Force service would get me GI benefits that I could use to pay for college. But how on earth could I go to college and leave my mother suffering from diabetes, and without adequate income to support her?

Several pivotal events occurred during my senior year of high school. I was an average student and managed to keep my grades up enough to graduate on time. In addition, my attraction to females was robust during these days, as expected for any seventeen-year-old boy. With no older male influence around me at the time, one thing led to another. I had to learn about romance and relationships on my own, from friends, or through love songs. During my senior year of high school, I soon found out I was a father-to-be. Thereafter, I spent many days and nights wondering how in the world I would manage having a child before I could even support myself. This experience forced me to "man up" and face the consequences of dealing with grown-up issues.

By the grace of God, music provided me answers. There's something about certain songs or music that mellows me out even in the midst of trying times. "Our Day Will Come" by Isaac Hayes is a song about a young man going off to the military and leaving his girl behind. The song "Too Late to Turn Back Now" by Cornelius

Brothers and Sister Rose also captured the essence of my life during this time. Yet another song from my high school graduation day that stuck with me was "We've Only Just Begun" by the Carpenters.

In the fall of 1971, my brother Kirby had gotten out of the Air Force and relocated to Atlanta. I would take a Trailways bus to Atlanta to visit him, and on Saturdays, he would ride me all around the city in his souped-up 1968 Pontiac GTO. That was how I learned my way around Atlanta and decided this was where I would live later in life. It was good to have him around because he always looked out for me. After school and on weekends, I worked for the local Piggly Wiggly store in Americus as a bagger in the months prior to graduation while my good friend Alphonson Baker worked in the produce department. Baker and I became lifelong friends due to us being like-minded and easygoing.

That bagger job was more motivation to join the Air Force. So, I got my mother to sign papers allowing me to enlist in the Delayed Enlistment Program before my eighteenth birthday. This allowed me to start my military commitment while completing my high school education.

My mother is the only parent I have ever known. All of my grandparents were dead before I was born. She struggled daily and endured tremendous hardships in her life. She never had a chance to get a decent education or have a decent job. The weight of the world almost broke her and perhaps I drew strength from watching her deal with her trials and tribulations. Despite her flaws, I willfully sacrificed my hopes and dreams by delaying the pursuit of a college degree in order to figure out a way to help support her.

In June of 1972, I graduated from Americus High School, and on July 5, 1972, I began basic military training at Lackland Air Force Base in San Antonio, Texas. The events of 1972 and the birth of my son Curtis Bernard Wright in July 1972 were living proof that it was too late to turn back; everything that happens has to happen. The inspiration for my first son's name came from singer Curtis Mayfield, who produced many soulful musical works in the '60s and '70s. Many thanks to his mom, Jo Anne Wright, for birthing and raising our son, who has become a responsible husband and parent, and thanks to my daughter-in-law Tramicha, who has given us some wonderful grandchildren.

Off to Air Force Training and Moody Air Force Base

ON JULY 4, 1972, I left Americus for the Armed Forces Examining and Entrance Station in Jacksonville, Florida. I can remember the fireworks going off into the nighttime sky as I spent my very first night alone in a hotel room awaiting processing. That night I wrote a letter to my mother expressing my gratitude to her and telling her I felt like I was becoming a man. The next day I was on a flight from Jacksonville to Atlanta and on to San Antonio to begin basic training. This was my first time in an airplane. I recall the excitement I felt as that Eastern Airlines jet took off from Jacksonville, headed to Atlanta for a stopover, and then on to San Antonio.

As we inductees arrived at Lackland AFB, a foul-mouthed, mean-ass drill sergeant came on the bus cussing and fussing about what we were going to do for the next six weeks in the oppressive Texas heat. After getting over the shock of being tormented and verbally abused, I slowly adapted to being stuck for four years with no idea where in the world I would end up. We were organized into groups of about fifty airmen in what the Air Force called flights. About a week into my training, we were standing in formation and another flight of airmen marched up next to our flight. To my delight, as I glanced at the other flight, I saw Charlie Fuller, who had been one of my high school classmates. I had no idea he had enlisted in the Air Force, and it would be many years before I would see him again.

Air Force basic training was initially about imposed discipline with a gradual transition to self-discipline. The imposed discipline was meant to weed out those who had no business being in the military. Staff Sergeant Robinson was our training instructor who had a passion for marching us around. As I recall, we marched in formation around the base, and our boots would simultaneously hit the ground step by step in perfect rhythm. I can still hear him barking out commands, "Lean back! Strut! Set 'em in!"

The assistant training instructor, Airman First Class Burton, was a slender Black guy who was sharp as a tack. One day as I was standing in formation, he sashayed up to me and said, "You think I like you, don't you?" to which I replied, "Yes, sir!" He then swiftly grabbed my sleeve to show me I had a button undone, which was a major mistake for a basic trainee to make. All in all, I enjoyed the training, which included learning about teamwork, physical fitness, neatness, marching, shooting an M-16 rifle, completing a challenging obstacle course, and following orders, as well as understanding military rules and regulations.

Around the middle of August, I completed basic training and transferred to Sheppard Air Force Base in Wichita Falls, Texas. Here was the place for me to learn how to repair and maintain military jet aircraft with one or two engines. The training began with a heavy emphasis on safety. For three months, I learned how to do routine tasks like changing tires, batteries, bulbs, servicing engine oil or hydraulics, and refueling jets. During my training, I learned that I would be assigned to Moody AFB in Valdosta, Georgia, which was the same place I had gone to take one of the many AFOQT tests about a year before. When I finished the course, I had had enough of Texas to last me a lifetime. Texas was like a foreign country to me because it was so different from where I grew up. I completed technical school and returned home on leave for two weeks in November 1972.

Around the middle of November, I took a Trailways bus from Americus to Valdosta to report for duty at Moody AFB. Being stationed at Moody was the perfect place for me because it was a pilot training base and I wanted to be a pilot. I vividly remember seeing the T-37 and T-38 trainer jets flying around the traffic pattern overhead every day. The sounds of jet engines were like music to my ears. The people were friendly and I cultivated numerous lifelong friendships during the remainder of my four-year enlistment. The popular hit song "Me and Mrs. Jones" by Billy Paul was out then, and I soon had a stereo record player to play it on. Fortunately for me, Sgt. Robert "Pop" Weaver was assigned as my trainer. Pop was a sharp, smooth-talking soul brother from South Georgia who took me under his wing and taught me much more than how to be an Air Force crew chief on the flight line.

One day Pop asked me if I was ready to marshal a returning aircraft into the parking spot. I told him I didn't think I was but decided to give it a try. As I stood on the spot where the nosewheel of T-38 was to come to a stop, the long-pointed pitot tube slowly came into view, headed for my chest. Instinctively, I was supposed to back up as I marshalled the aircraft into the parking spot, and when I didn't do as expected, Pop snatched me out of the way just in the nick of time. Once again, I was eternally grateful to have a savior by my side just like Alvin saving me from drowning.

Visiting Americus in front of my first car

Soon, I was launching, recovering, and servicing T-38s on my own, and ultimately managed other crew chiefs. In 1973, I got tired of walking and managed to scrape up four hundred dollars to buy an old brown stick-shift Pontiac Lemans with an engine that had a bad lifter that ticked all the time. Nevertheless, that car was still reliable and never let me down. My first roommate was John Young, who was from DC, which was the nickname he would be given. DC was a cool brother who always seemed to be mellowed out, if you know what I mean. He started calling me "Jay" and later in life I would give my middle son that nickname because I liked the sound of it. Meanwhile, I completed the necessary paperwork to make my ailing mother my military dependent. Thanks to the Air Force, my mother was able to get much-needed medical attention at Fort McPherson in Atlanta, where she had moved to live with my sister Elizabeth. With the benefit of me having extra military dependent pay, she was able to buy food at the military commissary, which saved my family a lot of money. By the grace of God, I was finally able to help my mother overcome some of the weight on her. The sacrifice of foregoing college to help her was well worth the wait.

Our family endured some sad times as well back in 1973. My nephew Glen Floyd was killed in a car accident near Poughkeepsie, New York, late in the year. He was just a young teenager, with so much life ahead of him. He is buried on the campus of the West Point Military Academy in New York. In Atlanta, my cousin Betty Bogan Few died suddenly that same year. Cousin Betty was a graduate of Clark College and a teacher in the Atlanta public schools. Clark College would later become my school of choice when I got out of the Air Force to attend college.

My second roommate was Larry Henderson, who was yet another person from Philadelphia. Somebody started calling him Leroy for some reason, and boy, did that nickname stick! He was the absolute best roommate a guy could ask for. Neither one of us smoked or drank, and we enjoyed the same kind of music. Thanks to Larry, I was able to enjoy some of the greatest soul music ever recorded straight out of Philly, a music city. Days working on the flight line were busy as we launched and recovered T-38 jets going out on training missions. In the summertime it was hot as hell on the flight line, and we had to deal with mosquitoes while working at night. In the wintertime, we had to work in the freezing cold some mornings and nights.

Thinking about the challenges I had trying to get commissioned as an Air Force officer, it was no surprise I didn't see but one or two Black instructor pilots or students training at Moody. One particularly friendly white instructor pilot named Chris Smisson often came out to fly one of the T-38s in my section on the flight line. While most instructor pilots paid me little attention, Chris Smisson took an active interest in me. He would always engage me in conversation and ask about my ambitions. After I told him I wanted to be an Air Force pilot, too, he always encouraged me to pursue my dreams. He will never know just how much that encouragement motivated me.

One highlight of my enlistment was getting to do a taxi ride in a T-38 with my supervisor out to an area to do something called a compass swing. Slowly but surely, I was gaining tidbits of experience that would benefit me years later and lift my burdens. During my entire enlistment, I continued to pursue every opportunity to take and pass the AFOQT, a difficult test that stood between me and the ability to become an Air Force officer. When not working the flight line during the week, Larry and I thoroughly enjoyed listening to good soul music or watching *Sanford and Son* on TV.

During the early '70s, there were a lot of things going on in the world that impacted Black people, and me in particular. Richard Nixon was in his second term as president when, ultimately, he got impeached and left office in shame for being a no-good crook. Due to ignorance on my part, I fell for a promise by Nixon to give military servicemen a pay raise. This was the first, last, and only time I have ever voted for a Republican for president. Unbeknownst to me, the Republican Party had begun to adopt blatant racist policies that would later prove to be extremely harmful to me and my people.

The Vietnam War was still going on. Thanks to the outspoken comedian and activist Dick Gregory, I learned a lot about the crimes Nixon and coconspirators had committed. This is why my generation knew how bad Donald Trump would be as a president and why he needed to be impeached in 2019. Gas prices escalated and, for a while, there were gas shortages throughout the country due to an oil embargo. During these days, musical works like "What the World Is Coming To" by Dexter Wansel provided me with some soothing, fantastic instrumental sounds accompanied by the periodic background noise of children playing. Dexter was an essential part of the outstanding musical group MFSB, which stands for Mother, Father, Sister, Brother. This Philadelphia international group provided a lot of great music for groups like the O'Jays, Billy Paul, Jerry Butler, Harold Melvin and the Blue Notes, Jean Carne, and numerous others.

Unity and Black pride among brothers was very strong in the military at that time. Some guys would participate in extensive handshakes or the greeting called dap, but at the very least you felt obligated to raise your clenched Black fist anytime you passed another brother on base. If you didn't give your fellow brother the recognition he was looking for, you were ostracized.

Since I had most weekends off, I would travel to Americus or Atlanta to visit family and friends. A good friend from Columbus, Georgia, named Donald Smith had a super-fast blue Roadrunner with a horn that said "meep meep," and before I got my car, we would travel together first to Americus and later on we would travel to Atlanta after my family relocated there. My sisters and our mother ended up living in two separate apartment units across the hall from each other in southwest Atlanta. It was always good to get away from the base and enjoy time in the big city. It also gave me a chance to visit the Atlanta University Center to explore the campus life I would later experience. And visits to Greenbriar Mall, where I could be around a multitude of Black people, were like heaven to me.

During my off time, I hung out with some of my fellow Black airmen. Lewis Carswell was one of my greatest Air Force buddies. He had a lime-green Dodge Duster with a black vinyl top and a six-pack carburetor sticking up through the hood. One night, Lewis got me to ride with him to downtown Valdosta. He wheeled through the front gate onto Bemis Road and floored that Duster. Before I knew it, we were hauling ass down the Bemis Road in excess of 120 mph, and I didn't even have on my seatbelt. This is when I came to understand what "There by the grace of God go I" means. Most of all, you could always depend on Lewis for some good Richard Pryor imitations and fun times.

Also around that time, I was hospitalized with the mumps after getting ill and going to sick call one morning. So far, by the grace of God, I haven't been hospitalized but once since then. Because I worked outside on the flight line, I developed serious allergies that kept me going to sick call often. My allergies were essentially cured when the doctor who examined me sent me to Fort Gordon in Augusta, Georgia, for an extensive evaluation. The cure involved taking an allergy shot each week at the Moody AFB hospital for a year. I am amazed and grateful that I haven't had any serious allergy issues since then.

After my relationship with Curtis's mother ended, my life was out of balance and filled with loneliness. I always knew how difficult a long-distance relationship could be, and it was best for both of us to move on. Ultimately, I found myself searching for someone in the nearby Valdosta area to hopefully have a steady relationship with. I would visit with my son Curtis from time to time, but because of the distance between us, it would take years for us to get close. One thing I did discover about Curtis and me was that we seemed to be a lot alike in personality. He's witty, cool, and levelheaded like me, and I am sure that has served him well in life.

Through introspection, I discovered that finding the ideal female companion was absolutely essential to having a happy and balanced life. One of my favorite songs during this time was "I've Got So Much to Give" by Barry White. That song summed up my feelings about finding that one special lady who would provide the balance I needed for a well-rounded life. Yet I soon discovered that finding a suitable mate was extremely difficult because of the hidden psychological damage done to our people, including me. At times, repressed feelings of resentment toward entrenched institutional racism would surface. I spent many days pondering why Black people have been treated so badly for so long.

Napping after working the graveyard shift on the flightline

On top of that, I wondered why my relationships with women were so difficult or unstable. I would later learn that many relationships between Black men and women were stormy due to the stress of racism and despair. Some Black men even took their frustrations out on those closest to them. That's why the Earth Wind & Fire song "Feelin' Blue" became so special to me. Ironically, my roommate Larry had taken a picture of me sleeping in a chair after I had been working all night on the flight line. There is a befitting lyric in that song that asks, "Why do you sleep in a chair?" and answers saying there's not much to do when you're feeling blue. Another comforting song was "Four Cornered Room" by the group called War. This song meant a lot because I sat alone in that four-cornered room on Moody Air Force Base thinking a lot and planning for my future. There was so much I needed to learn about myself and about women before I would have any chance at having a successful relationship.

So many other talented soul music artists and groups produced the songs I needed to cope with whatever situation I was dealing with. Essentially, soul music of the '70s was therapy for me. Needless to say, "Living for the Weekend" was a favorite song by the O'Jays that reflected the ongoing happenings at the NCO Club on soul nights or the weekend parties I attended. A two-year relationship with a lady from Valdosta was promising but ended due to compatibility issues. During that time, I had another near fatal mishap when I fell asleep returning from Tifton, Georgia, after visiting her. The Marvin Gaye song "If I Should Die Tonight" comes to mind when I remember nearly hitting a parked tractor-trailer truck while driving south on I-75 near Adel. Ironically, years later in 1981, my Aunt Nola Mae Whitehead died in a tragic chain-reaction accident not too far from that location.

Around this time Marvin Gaye songs like "God Is Love" and "Wholy Holy" revived my interest in religion. These inspirational songs plus the Earth, Wind & Fire songs "Keep Your Head to the

Sky" and "Open Our Eyes" actually began to open my eyes. In order to get through life, I wisely realized I needed some help; I needed to develop a closer relationship with the God, who had twice saved me from a near-death experience! Over time, this quest for a closer relationship with God would lead me to religion, the next vital step toward spirituality.

On another trip to Tifton on a backroad through Nashville, Georgia, I had a dangerous encounter with a mean ole white racist Georgia state trooper. I've never had a fast car like many of my buddies. Nevertheless, while driving about sixty miles per hour on that dark backroad, I was pulled over by the state trooper for speeding. By the grace of God, I found a safe place to pull over with witnesses around. After I pulled over and stopped in front of a store, he angrily approached my car and asked why I didn't pull over when he first turned on the blue lights. And he really didn't like me saying I didn't think it was safe to pull over back there because of the sharp drop-off along that part of the road. When he asked me how fast I was going, I replied about fifty-five miles per hour. Then he said, "We're going to say you was doing ninety!"

I glanced up at this big-ass white man in his nice blue-and-grey Georgia state trooper uniform with a big badge and a big gun, and carefully assessed my situation. Recognizing I was at a distinct disadvantage, I humbly said, "If you say I was doing ninety, then I must have been doing ninety."

He wrote up the speeding ticket and made me follow him back to Nashville, Georgia, to the justice of the peace office. Fortunately, I always carried some extra "emergency money" whenever I traveled. So, I had enough cash to pay the fifty-dollar fine on the spot and I was free to go. That ticket never showed up on my driving record, perhaps because the state trooper and the guy in the justice of the peace office spilt my fine. Most notably, I could have proven that my old brown Pontiac Lemans wouldn't do ninety going downhill, because that clunker had an annoying bad lifter in the engine. Instead of getting all upset, I chalked it up to driving while Black and let it go, like so many other episodes of overt or covert racism.

I had learned a long time ago that sometimes you get into situations that humble you so you can face reality head on. On base, the only trouble I ever got into was getting caught in a random vehicle search as I was leaving the base with a pellet gun under the seat of my car that looked like a real .357-caliber pistol. The military does not allow individuals to have private weapons of any kind on base and I knew better. Even before my commander could find out about the incident, I went to his office to plead for forgiveness. Fortunately, this was the only time I ever came close to being in any kind of trouble.

As I've said repeatedly, good music has helped me through some tough times. Songs like "Summer Madness" by Kool & The Gang were just what I needed to mellow me out. That's why I didn't need to drink alcohol or get high like some of the airmen I knew.

Having never been out west, I scheduled some military leave time and arranged to visit my childhood savior Alvin Bowen, who lived in Los Angeles after getting out of the Air Force around 1970. I drove up from Moody AFB to Robins AFB and caught a military hop on a C-141 Starlifter cargo jet headed to Norton AFB, California. This was to be my very first flight on a military aircraft. I wanted to visit the flight deck so badly, but the all-white flight crew didn't seem too friendly, so I just left that idea alone and enjoyed the ride in an airplane with virtually no windows. After arriving at Norton Air Force Base near San Bernardino, I emerged from the C-141 and started breathing some of the worst air I had ever seen. Yes, you could actually see the smog that settled in Southern California due to the pollution caused by cars and factories. In spite of my experience with the air, my visit with Alvin was awesome! He showed me around Los Angeles and treated me extremely well.

It was during that visit the repressed memory of being saved from drowning by Alvin came back to me. I said to Alvin, "You saved my life!" He just grinned and said, "Yes I did." Alvin had been an electrician in the Air Force, and it seemed nothing ever "shocked him." All I could do was say thanks and be filled with extreme gratitude to this giant of a man who humbly plucked a little Black drowning boy out of that nasty, snake-infested Muckalee Creek one day. I will never, ever be able to thank him enough.

My trip back to Moody AFB was a lot tougher. I caught another C-141 cargo jet from Norton AFB near Ontario, California, to McGuire AFB in New Jersey. There I sat for about two days sleeping in the terminal because there weren't any flights going near Georgia. Thereafter, I was able to catch a C-9 medical airlift airplane headed for Cherry Point Marine Corp Base in Jacksonville, North Carolina. Once I got to that God-forsaken place, I was stuck because there were absolutely no military flights I could catch headed anywhere near Georgia. So, I had no choice but to catch a bus all the way back to Warner Robins. Who knows how long that took. I don't care to remember. I was just glad to get back to that old, worn-out brown Pontiac Lemans I had left parked at Robins AFB.

The friendships created at Moody were priceless. Meeting and getting to know Walter "Andy" Andrews was a real treasure for me. Andy, originally from Atlanta, was reassigned from the Philippines to Moody somewhere around 1973 and we worked in the same flight together. Andy was a tough, no-nonsense brother who garnered the utmost respect from everyone and didn't take no crap whatsoever. One day, he encouraged me to go with him to hear comedian-turned-activist Dick Gregory speak at Valdosta State University. Thanks to Andy, Dick Gregory became one of my heroes because he was the most outspoken Black civil rights activist and comic I had ever seen in person. The song "That's the Way of the World" by Earth, Wind & Fire reminds me of that point in life when I was coming to grips with reality.

Every now and then, several of the brothers in the dorm would gather in our room to sit around listening to Richard Pryor albums or soul music and talking trash. Then there were times we would go to parties where songs like "Give Up the Funk" and "P-Funk" by Funkadelic were playing. Those were some of the best times I've ever had. Unfortunately, a tragic event occurred when a brother from another dorm was working in the cockpit of a T-38 on the flight line. Somehow, he triggered the ejection seat and was killed. About twenty of us brothers attended his funeral near Augusta and wore our military uniforms as a show of support. His family was so delighted to see us, and we were glad to give them some comfort.

At some point, I took a karate class at Valdosta State College to satisfy my desire to learn martial arts. Although I never advanced to higher levels, the confidence in knowing how to defend myself was uplifting. I also got enough courage to go to the base pool and actually teach myself how to swim. Prior to that, the fear of drowning had kept me from learning how, but I never liked being afraid of anything. All it took was having a lifeguard who could hopefully save me if need be. Initially, I hung on to the side near the deep part of the pool while learning how to tread water. Once I felt confident that I could tread water, I ventured into deep water swimming near the side until my confidence became stronger. Then I would force myself down to the bottom of the pool to see how long I could stay there, and then spring off the pool bottom back to the top to tread water again or hang on to the side. Before long, I was swimming the length of the pool and diving off the high diving board. With the benefit of having access to a public swimming pool, I was able to learn to swim on my very own after almost drowning years ago in a filthy, snake-infested creek in Americus. How times had changed! I was glad I had overcome the inability to swim, another thing that had almost killed me.

After getting tired of that sorry Lemans, I traded it in for a beautiful triple black 1973 Oldsmobile Cutlass Supreme. I named that car the EXPRESS because of my trips up and down I-75 where I would see busses labeled "EXPRESS." On top of that, the music group B. T. Express came out with a song called "Express"; I used that name as my CB radio handle as well. Sensing a need to have a document that defined who I was, I drafted a very special document entitled JOHNNIE on August 7, 1974. In this valuable decree, I explained how I had adopted a cool state of mind and was dedicated to approaching life realistically with all of its ups and downs. This approach would serve me well over the next few decades.

JOHNNIE

> *I am a wise, liberal and precise Black man serious as hell about my life and how I live it. I arose and developed from childhood into manhood learning mainly from experience and the will to understand. I am a man of many misfortunes, hard times and know loneliness as a friend. It is through these misfortunes, hard times and lonely hours I have come to understand life. There is some good in all bad, and bad in all good. It is also through these toils and strife I established a basis for foundation. I live in a world all my own which is very natural and actual. My world is simply REALITY, its ups and downs; its heaven, its hell; its love and its hatred. In this world*

I seek HAPPINESS but without expectation; I aspire to achieve but remain prepared for failure. I believe in FACTS yet remain open-minded to fantasy. I strive to change that I can and calmly accept that I cannot for I am a man of great PATIENCE and UNDERSTANDING. I believe in do unto as have done unto me. I know LOVE as devoted affection and care; I can be as bad and as destructive as made be yet as nice and good as allowed. I do nothing without reason. I am observant of my environment and reserve to the knowledge I behold. These facts and principles govern my action and it is upon this foundation along with experience that I live my life in its entirety dedicated to FACTS and a COOL state of mind.

Johnnie E. Jones Jr.
August 7, 1974

Standing in front of a T-38 and F4E

During the summer of 1975, I met a female intern working at Moody and she was a student at Clark College. We stayed in touch, and because of her I was convinced Clark College was the place for me to get my college education. The Temptations song "Memories" reminds me of that day and time. In the fall of 1975, my buddy Keith Harris from Miami encouraged me to go to a FAMU football game. That night, we went to an amazing nightclub called the

Electric Eye. I will never forget the unique lighted dance floor, which made you want to dance the night away. The Ohio Players had just come out with the song "Sweet Sticky Thing." Later that year, Moody AFB was transitioning from an Air Training Command T-37/T-38 base to a Tactical Air Command F-4 Phantom base. That fall, I got orders to transfer to Luke AFB in Phoenix, Arizona, and was to report to base around January 1976. So, I went to Atlanta on leave to visit with family before I was to drive out to Phoenix. While I was in Atlanta, I ran into an airman I knew from Moody who worked in personnel. He told me I could stay at Moody AFB until the end of my enlistment if I wanted to. So, I got reassigned to Moody, packed up my stuff, and headed back to the base to serve out the rest of my enlistment.

The spring of 1976 proved to be a very pivotal time of my life. The song by Rufus and Chaka Khan "Sweet Thing" comes to mind when I think of another romantic relationship that ended as I neared the end of my enlistment. This occurred after my brother Kirby and his fiancée Lucille had gotten married in April of 1976. I had hoped my "sweet thing" would be the one, but she had other plans. That same month, my unit sent me to MacDill AFB in Tampa, Florida, for three weeks to attend systems school on the F-4. I returned to Moody and went to work as a fully qualified F-4 Phantom crew chief, the same type of aircraft I had seen the Thunderbirds fly beyond the speed of sound at Robins AFB.

The F-4s came to Moody from Thailand, where they had been used in the Vietnam War. These returning fighter jets had to be thoroughly inspected because sometimes drugs would be smuggled from Thailand underneath panels on these jets. One of my early tasks working on this jet was to remove numerous panels, which meant undoing hundreds of screws to get the panels off. Working on the F-4E was a dangerous and nasty job. At the end of my shift, I would smell like a combination of jet fuel, hydraulic fuel, and plain ole flight line funk. This was further motivation for me to leave active duty, move to Atlanta, and attend Clark College in the fall to pursue my dream.

As my relationship with that "sweet thing" faded, there was nothing to keep me at Moody. "Morning Tears" by the group MFSB will always remind me of that sad time when I knew I had to move on with my life. The song entitled "Coldest Days of My Life" also came to remind me of this period when I had to face the reality that some things are just not meant to be. This was the beginning of my acceptance that everything that happens has to happen. I had already decided I would leave the Air Force in July 1976 at the end of my enlistment and enroll in Clark College that fall. I had finally moved off base with the same guy, Jimmy Summerlin, who had told me about the option to stay at Moody instead of transferring to Luke AFB.

Because I jumped at any chance to become an Air Force flight crewmember, I took advantage of the opportunity to sign on as an Air Force Reservist at Charleston AFB to become a C-141 flight engineer. Now, the C-141 Starlifter was a beautiful white-and-gray four-engine jet cargo aircraft I had seen flying in and out of Moody every now and then. It was also the same type aircraft I caught a ride on a couple of years ago to Norton AFB, California, to visit my good friend and childhood savior, Alvin Bowen. The only problem was that going to C-141 school beyond the summer of '76 would make finishing college in four years very difficult. Nevertheless, I was just glad to finally be assigned to a flying unit. As July 4, 1976, approached, I took terminal leave from Moody so I could go to Atlanta and find a job for the summer. With my Cutlass Supreme packed with all my worldly possessions, I put Valdosta and Moody Air Force Base in my rearview mirror and headed north up I-75 to the ATL for good.

The Jet Will Fly!

Left to right is Lewis Carswell, Robert P. Weaver, Larry Henderson, Henry Bunn, Melvin Sessions and myself as we retired Airmen who served together at Moody AFB Georgia in the 70's came together at Robins AFB Georgia on Veteran's Day 2023. The statue is of Eugene Jacques Bullard, born in Columbus Georgia, who was the first Black pilot who flew for France in WWI. Bullard's statue was recently erected at the Robins Museum of Aviation.

On to Atlanta and Clark College

THE SUMMER OF 1976 proved to be a pivotal time in my life. I was fresh off active duty with nothing material to speak of but a fairly nice car and a big dream to become an Air Force pilot. I had very little money and a tremendous amount of faith in myself. Kirby and Lucille were newlyweds and gracious enough to allow me to live with them until I could get my own place to live. But hard as I tried, I couldn't find a job anywhere. Fortunately, the 701st Military Airlift Squadron I was assigned to at Charleston AFB in South Carolina allowed me to do two weeks of paid active duty in July of that year.

On the way to Charleston, I met up with my nephew Joseph Floyd Jr. in Macon and we had a blast attending an Earth, Wind & Fire concert at the Macon Coliseum. EWF is one of my favorite music groups, and they put on the best concerts I have ever seen in my life. Charleston has always been one of my favorite places to visit, and I had a great time while I was there. Continuing to serve as a reservist was the best decision I could make because it gave me a way to enjoy the best of serving in the military and being a civilian at the same time. As I drove back home from Charleston that summer, the transmission in my car began to slip badly. I was fortunate I made it all the way back to Atlanta.

When I got back to Atlanta, the transmission needed to be rebuilt and I didn't have the four hundred dollars to get it fixed. Lucky for me, my dear, sweet sister Elizabeth loaned me the money, and soon I was back on the road again. As a weekend warrior based at Charleston AFB but living in Atlanta, I would get on a C-141 cargo jet once a month at Dobbins AFB in Marietta on a Friday afternoon. That airplane would make several stops in Florida picking up other reservists and taking us to Charleston AFB for our weekend duty. On the Sunday after completing reserve duty, that C-141 reservist shuttle would take us back to our respective cities or bases near our homes.

My reserve unit had notified me that I was scheduled to attend C-141 flight engineer school at Altus AFB in Oklahoma in late September. I was extremely excited to finally become a flight crewmember. On the other hand, completing a four-year college degree in four years had just become much more difficult. In August of 1976, Hurricane Belle was threatening the Atlantic Coast, and the C-141 reservist shuttle was cancelled. Unbeknownst to me, I was expected to drive to Charleston AFB to attend that regularly scheduled monthly Unit Training Assembly (UTA) weekend. After missing that weekend of duty, my unit commander sent me a nasty letter that really pissed me off. I responded with a letter telling them to send my military records to the Air Reserve Personnel Center

(ARPC) in Denver, and I planned to serve out the remainder of my six-year military and reserve obligation in the inactive reserves, which didn't require any connection to an active unit.

Little did I know God was again ordering my steps, or should I say altering my steps, to allow me to achieve my dream of becoming an Air Force pilot. In the meantime, Clark College had accepted me as a student in the class of 1980 starting in the fall of 1976. The Veteran's Administration (VA) GI Benefit program paid me directly, so I was able to pay my bills. After attending orientation in September, I began classes while still living with Kirby and Lucille. As planned, I bravely selected computer science as my major. Once I had enough money coming in to get a place of my own, I rented an efficiency unit at Franciscan Apartments in Southwest Atlanta with all utilities included. It was the cheapest place I could find that was in a fairly decent area, and I enjoyed living in that small space.

Kirby gave me an old bed he had, and I built a table to eat on and do my homework. It felt good to finally have a place all to myself. Curtis's mom relocated to Atlanta during this time, and periodically, I would spend time with Curtis as he and I tried to figure out how to communicate better. Around this time, Jimmy Carter had just been elected as president, and I recall going to a victory celebration for him in downtown Atlanta. It was a great time to be in Atlanta because a Black man, Maynard Jackson, had also previously been elected as the first Black mayor of the city. The song "Chocolate City" by Parliament-Funkadelic comes to mind when I think of coming to Atlanta to live and go to college.

In the spring of 1977, I began to really miss being around airplanes and being associated with the Air Force. Around that time, an event at Dobbins AFB was held to recruit people into the various units at that base. When I told the recruiter I wanted to get into a flying unit, he introduced me to Major Bob Holden and others at the 700th Tactical Airlift Squadron. To my surprise, this Air Force Reserve unit was flying C-7 Caribous, which were the same kind of airplanes I used to see flying near Eastview Elementary School in Americus in the early '60s. What was even more amazing was the fact that there were three Black pilots in the unit: Carl Gamble, John Bailey, and Chris Franks. Carl was a pilot for Piedmont Airlines, and John and Chris were Delta pilots. Eventually, there was one other Black flight mechanic named George Frazier. George worked for Lockheed and was to become someone I appreciated hanging around too. After joining the unit, I underwent On The Job Training (OJT) as a C-7 Caribou flight mechanic, which entailed servicing, preflighting, and loading and unloading the aircraft as well as inflight and airdrop duties.

When I first joined the unit, I thought I wouldn't be able to tolerate being around all these white folks in Cobb County, which was a lily-white area with a racist history. But, to my surprise, even though I was definitely in the minority, my fellow white airmen treated me well and I actually came to enjoy being around them because they joked and poked fun at each other just like Black folks do.

Having finished my first year of college, I flew on a commercial airline flight to Fairchild AFB in Spokane, Washington, to attend land survival school. I later flew on a commercial airline flight to Miami to attend water survival school at Homestead AFB in Homestead, Florida. My fondest memory of this training was parasailing in Biscayne Bay and being released to land in the water as if I had bailed out of an airplane. Due to a strong wind that day, I hit the water so hard it damn near knocked the wind out of me. In addition, I had to make sure the parachute didn't cover my head as I prepared myself to be rescued.

Being at Clark College and the Atlanta University Center was like being in heaven, because I loved being around beautiful Black people. "Love Ballad" by L.T.D. and Jeffrey Osborne was the hit song of that time. There at Clark I met lifelong friends, like Greg Nash and Clarence Johnson. After a few relationships that went nowhere, I met and fell in love with Thelma Devoe, who was a student at Morris Brown College. Thelma and I spent lots of time together, and once again, I found myself a father-to-be. Even though I had only known her less than a year, we ultimately decided to get married, set out to pursue our careers, and raise a family.

Serving as a flight mechanic on the C-7A Caribou

In May 1978, I was a part of a C-7 crew that participated in a fly-in to honor the Tuskegee Airmen and Black aviators at Tuskegee's Moten Field. This event provided me with more motivation to become an Air Force officer pilot. Being a C-7 flight mechanic was a great way to transition into flying. The US Army previously used those old high-wing cargo airplanes with two reciprocating engines before they were transferred to the Air Force in the early '60s. The Air Force had used them in Vietnam, and some of the pilots in my unit had flown the C-7 in actual combat conditions. Usually, about once a month, I would take weekend cross-country missions to places like MacDill AFB or Eglin AFB in Florida. Most trips were either airdrop or aeromedical missions. The airplane was unpressurized and did not have an autopilot. Nearly all of my cross-country trips were with white pilots and most of them treated me with respect. On several long flights when one pilot wanted a break from sitting in the pilot seat, I was allowed to sit in their place. Of course, this unauthorized occupancy of a pilot seat by me, an enlisted flight mechanic, was my very first opportunity to fly an airplane. I will always be grateful to those pilots who allowed me to fly straight and level for a few minutes. That experience was a welcomed opportunity to get a feel of what it takes to actually fly an airplane.

On each flight sitting in the cargo compartment, I gradually learned little tidbits of information about flying airplanes. I recall standing in between the pilot seats as they flew approaches to various runways. I even picked up a valuable lesson on how to land when Major Holden was giving instruction to Lieutenant Barry Fuller, who was new to the airplane. "Aim point and airspeed" were the words that stuck with me during that flight. This was the technique I would use throughout my flying career as a pilot. Perhaps the most exciting Air Force Reserve trip I had was to Atlantic City around 1979 when we participated in a popular airshow. Before the Air Force Thunderbird demonstration team flew that day, my C-7 crew flew the Army Golden Knights precision parachute team over Atlantic City Beach, where they jumped out of our aircraft to land on the beachfront. It was an exciting trip because I got to see Atlantic City when it was a thriving city with several casinos.

After we had done our airdrops, we returned to the hotel

where we were staying that afternoon. My pilot was Captain Bill Jackson, who had a deep Southern drawl and loved teasing everybody. Each of the three of us crewmembers had our own rental car. Bill had returned to the hotel first, and as I arrived, I saw him in a room full of Black folks who had gathered for the airshow. While walking past that room full of black folks, I heard Bill say with that deep Southern drawl, "Come on in, Johnnie." I entered the room and was greeted by everyone like I was a hero. These Black folks had every kind of liquor you can think of, and everybody was feeling tipsy. Bill had a mixed drink in his hand, and somebody asked me what kind of drink I wanted. I stated that I did not drink alcohol, but they weren't hearing it. Upon their insistence that I have a drink, I said, "Give me a screwdriver," which I knew included orange juice and vodka. Needless to say, I wound up getting drunk for the very first time in my life, thanks to Bill Jackson, who was the last person I had expected to see in a room full of Black folks.

That eventful evening left me lying on my hotel bed, which seemed to be spinning around and around, before Bill coerced me to go to the hotel restaurant to eat at the buffet. That, my friends, was a very bad idea, and you can imagine what happened after that. My initiation into being a full-fledged Air Force flight crewmember was now complete. Thankfully, I would eventually learn to drink responsibly over time, among other lessons. One very unique and important lesson I learned from flying came from sitting in the cargo compartment for hours watching that propeller rotating around and around at 2,700 revolutions per minute. Most notably, I realized a rotating propeller is sort of like life. As the world spins around and around, everything on or around it depends on balance, just like that propeller. If that propeller doesn't stay perfectly balanced it could come off of that engine with disastrous consequences. The same is true in life. Without balance, your life can literally come apart—as I would come to find out. I have always tried to maintain a healthy work/life balance, but it has never been easy. As a matter of fact, balance also has a lot to do with getting an airplane to fly and to keep it flying. In order to overcome the weight of the world, get airborne, and keep from crashing, a pilot needs to adhere to strict weight and balance limitations.

Because the apartments where I lived were for adults without children only, Thelma and I eventually had to move. We made the move to Deerfield Apartments on Campbellton Road in Atlanta around the middle of 1978 after we got married. I took a part-time job working for JC Penney in a stockroom, and I also worked at the VA office in downtown Atlanta. My computer science courses began to get increasingly difficult primarily due to one person, Grover Simmons. Mr. Simmons was head of the computer science department at Morehouse and you couldn't get a computer science degree without taking a class from him. Being the brave person I am, I took his class with five other students. Two students dropped the class after he humiliated them for not understanding the complex problems he presented. Because it was beyond the deadline to drop a class, and I was unable to obtain a passing grade and had endured as much humiliation as I could, I scheduled a one-on-one conference with Mr. Simmons. In the meeting, I cleverly and politely expressed my extreme distaste for his teaching style and his demoralizing tactics in a graphic way. He couldn't care less. Needless to say, I got an F in the two classes I was taking from him.

Being newlywed with a new baby boy on the way while working two part-time jobs and struggling as a college student left me with lots of weight on my shoulders. As God would have it, I somehow had a revelation. In order to get my life back in balance, something had to change. A consultation with my college counselor revealed that I could change my major to business administration and still graduate on time if I took classes during the summer. That was when I made plans to take summer school classes at Georgia State University every summer in order to graduate on time in 1980. After I changed my major to business administration, I met Ms. Jane Dawkins, one special college professor who taught me business communications. It was in her class I learned to write effective business letters. Another class I took allowed me to explore the development of a business idea I called Emergency Jet Service.

The objective of this business was to obtain a business jet and sign up thousands of people who were interested in the ability to obtain on-demand private jet transportation in emergency situations. It's an idea that still has potential and a great way to own a private jet. During this time, I got a pleasant surprise one evening. There was an unexpected knock at the door of our apartment. To my surprise, my old roommate Larry Henderson from Philadelphia had decided to come to Atlanta to pay me a visit. No other friend or roommate I had been associated with had ever contacted me or paid me a visit. That meant a whole lot to me, and I will never forget it. Larry remains one of my best friends today.

SSgt. Johnny Jo...   ...oungest recruit

Meanwhile, in October 1978, my second son, Johnnie Edward Jones III, was born on the night of a full moon. Johnnie—or Jay, as we called him—was a very active child. My decision to call him Jay originated from the fact that my first Air Force roommate, John "DC" Young, called me that name. I recall how it always took a bottle and a half of milk for Jay to be satisfied. Unlike anything I had ever seen before, Jay would take the milk bottle and throw it across the room, which signaled that he wanted more.

In between college classes, work, and reserve duty, my days were extremely busy. Time spent playing with my son Jay was a welcome relief from the drudgery of life. His unique giggling always made me laugh and will never be forgotten. I also managed to spend time with my first-born son, Curtis, whenever I could when his mother relocated to the Atlanta area. Curtis was quiet around me, and we continued to work on improving our relationship over time. Without the benefit of having a father in my life, I was left on my own to figure out how to become a good father, which is not something you can learn from reading a book.

Somewhere along the way around 1979, someone decided to steal my beloved Cutlass Supreme. I emerged from our apartment to go somewhere one morning and the best car I had ever owned was gone! The car was ultimately found stripped in Northwest

Atlanta near Hollywood Road, which was known to be a rough neighborhood. The insurance settlement only gave me enough money to buy a basic cheap Toyota Corolla with no radio or air conditioning. That little car would provide basic transportation for my family and me until I was able to buy a better car the next year.

Midway through my college days at Clark College, my education outside the classroom was just as important as what I learned in class. One important lesson was learning how to use critical thinking to make sound decisions or change course when necessary. Switching my major to business administration was one such decision that made it possible to graduate from college in four years. Fortunately, I found majoring in business administration to be much more suitable for me. My grades improved to As and Bs again, as they were in my early college years, and things were once again looking up. I learned a lot about business, which proved to be valuable knowledge as time went on.

At the urging of my fellow reservists at Dobbins AFB, including John Bailey, I took a discovery flight at Charlie Brown Airport in Fulton County Airport. This was my first chance to fly and land an airplane. Early in 1980, I started taking flying lessons when I found out about the ACE Academy run by Black pilots on the other side of the airport. My first instructor was Ozzie Ross, who was also an enlisted Air Force veteran with ambitions to be an airline pilot. After taking basic ground school courses, Ozzie took me up flying in a Cessna 150. Thereafter, I flew about once a week until I had about ten flight hours. We would practice approaches to stalls and recovery from a stall, as well as steep turns and other maneuvers.

When Ozzie wasn't available to fly with me, I flew with the legendary ACE Academy flight instructor Julius Alexander. Mr. Alexander was an outstanding pilot and loved teaching people how to fly airplanes. Mr. Alexander recently passed away but his lifelong work of teaching Black children about aviation and flying airplanes is legendary. Taking flight lessons was extremely expensive, so it was hard to fly more often. Nevertheless, the experience of knowing that I could fly an airplane was a terrific confidence booster. Also, I once again took the AFOQT in Atlanta, and this time I passed that difficult test that had been standing in my way for years. I thought the SAT was a hard test, but the AFOQT was clearly deliberately created to be hard in order to eliminate certain people like me. The credit goes to divine intervention for me passing that test. Why? Because an unusual thing happened during that test that allowed me the opportunity to pass after taking it four or five times. My JET WILL FLY motto was taking effect, because those words were ingrained into my subconsciousness and the universe began to work with me instead of against me.

Fortunately, I attended Georgia State University during the last two summers in order to take the courses I needed to graduate on time from Clark College. I took a management class as well managerial accounting and cost accounting classes. Ironically, classes at Clark College and Georgia State were like night and day. At Clark, we hardly ever had to read or cover every chapter in a textbook. On the contrary, a student at Georgia State was routinely expected to read multiple chapters overnight and be prepared for a test the next day. We read several textbooks cover to cover at Georgia State, and I learned a whole lot in a short time.

Nevertheless, getting a college degree from Clark taught me things I could never have learned at a predominantly white college. Classes at Clark taught by black instructors revealed knowledge I needed to cope with the systemic racism I was sure to face in the working world. Additionally, being in an exclusively Black institution of higher learning made me appreciate the intellect of my people, our history, and our culture. Lastly, the

Clark College motto of "Find a way or make one" was incidentally what I had been doing all my life.

I had found a way to get help for my mother, get a college degree, and I was finally about to find my way to become an Air Force pilot. In May 1980, I proudly graduated from Clark College with a bachelor's degree in business administration with a concentration in management. Fortunately, I had also taken enough computer science classes to get hired at Southern Bell, which was the major telephone company at that time. My nephew Bob Floyd was instrumental in getting me hired. He had come down from Connecticut to work as a computer programmer at Southern Bell a few years earlier. Sadly, Bob had a serious car accident in the summer of 1980 when the Triumph Spitfire he was driving overturned on the I-75/85 downtown connector. He spent most of August that year in a coma and eventually regained consciousness. The accident left Bob with some disability due to a brain injury and long-term memory loss. The Bob Floyd we knew was still alive but the injuries he suffered from the accident distorted his memory and his physical form to the point that he was not the same person that we knew before.

JC Penney also offered me a job as a COBOL programmer because I had worked at their catalogue center part time while I was in college. Incidentally, I turned them down because the position at Southern Bell paid more. My job at Southern Bell was initially at the Hurt Building in downtown Atlanta. Working as an assembler language programmer using the company's proprietary software, called Sobel, was not a desirable job. This particular programming language was not usable anywhere outside of Southern Bell. If I had the opportunity to train on the IBM computer system that used COBOL, I would have been much happier. In the meantime, I bought a brand-new copper-colored 1980 Toyota

Corolla SR5, which was one of the best cars I have ever owned. After completing all the requirements to apply to become an officer in the active-duty Air Force as well as in the Air Force Reserves, I patiently waited for an acceptance notification. During the fall of 1980, my acceptance notification came through for an active-duty officer and pilot training slot.

Now I had a real dilemma. Should I turn down the active-duty slot and hope the reserve slot would come through? This was a tough decision because accepting an active-duty slot would leave me open to being assigned anything the Air Force flies and being stationed anywhere in the world after training. I knew that I wanted to have as much control over my Air Force career, so I took a chance and opted to wait for the Air Force Reserve slot. A few weeks later, the Air Force Reserve slot came through and I was all set to start Officer Training School on December 15, 1980. To my amazement, members of my reserve unit pitched in and bought me a briefcase as a going-away present. I was pleasantly surprised and most appreciative. It was at this moment that my motto, THE JET WILL FLY, was driving my success. I would soon realize that in my mind failure was not an option and never entered into my subconscious. I was about to embark upon the adventures of a lifetime.

Becoming a Proud Air Force Officer and Pilot

THE PHOTO OF me in the previous chapter reflects the pride I have in becoming an Air Force officer and pilot. Wearing that beautiful blue Air Force uniform with those bright silver pilot wings meant I had set and achieved a momentous goal of a lifetime, a major goal that few people who look like me have successfully achieved. Glory to God!

In December of 1980, Thelma and I had just bought our very first house in College Park, a suburban area south of Atlanta. She was working for AT&T as a computer programmer in Alpharetta, Georgia. On December 14th I departed for San Antonio, Texas, to begin Officer Training School that next day. OTS was a compressed course designed to teach a civilian to be a military officer in three short months. It was my last option to become an Air

Force officer because I had long ago been essentially rejected for the Air Force Academy and an AFROTC scholarship. Upon arrival at OTS, I was introduced to my instructor, Lieutenant Maureen Clay. Lieutenant Clay was a no-nonsense, tough little lady officer who was stern and demanding. Her main message to her students was, "Pay attention to detail." Over the course of this training, she proceeded to whip her fourteen students into shape as Air Force officers. Of course, I was the one and only Black student in my OTS class. I learned to keep my room neat and spotless, march a formation of officer trainees, manage people, give presentations, write correspondences, and be a responsible military leader.

My prior enlisted experience proved to be valuable, as I was able to help my fellow students adapt to Air Force life. Sadly, in the middle of my training, tragedy struck when I got word that several of my family members had been involved in a deadly traffic accident near Adel, Georgia. My aunt Nola Mae, who lived in Dooly County, Georgia, had been killed when a tractor-trailer truck smashed into the car she was riding in on a foggy I-75. My mind was flooded with memories of the childhood trips from Americus to Unadilla in Dooly County to see Aunt Nola, Uncle T. W., and cousins. Aunt Nola was my mother's sister and one of the sweetest ladies I have ever known, and it was difficult to comprehend that she was gone. My mother was in another car that was struck as well but she was just shaken up. The two cars had been returning from a funeral in Florida when they drove into a combination of smoke and blinding fog that had rolled onto I-75 interstate highway. I flew home to attend the funeral and check on my mother. Lieutenant Clay was compassionate and accommodating to me, and that made a huge difference in helping me to complete my training.

Training included physical fitness, mostly in the form of jogging. There was a Roadrunner Program that required each student to run seven miles a week. One time I fell behind in my running, so I went out to the track one night and ran seven miles straight without stopping. I was going around and around that quarter-mile track for over an hour and a half.

There were some days when we had to go to an assembly of all the OTS students. Usually, some gung-ho officer would challenge us to quit if we didn't believe in our flag or fighting and dying for our country. Some days, memories of those times in elementary school made me want to quit because I knew in my mind that liberty and justice for all was still a myth. I used to call Kirby, who was working at Sears in Atlanta, and he would have to talk me out of quitting. When Kirby wasn't there, his friend Clarence Jordan or Gus Roberson would do the same. They would remind me that being successful in my goal to become an Air Force pilot was bigger than anything else. Thanks to their encouraging words, I redoubled my efforts and made it through the ups and downs of OTS.

In March 1981, I became a second lieutenant in the Air Force and returned home to College Park to prepare for a year of Undergraduate Pilot Training (UPT) at Columbus AFB in Columbus, Mississippi. Originally, I was supposed to go to Williams AFB in Phoenix, Arizona, but I had it changed so I wouldn't have to uproot my family and move them for a year. This would mean I would drive six hours home to Atlanta to see my wife and son every other weekend for a year.

Later in March of 1981, I drove over to Columbus AFB and reported for flight training. Entering UPT was the culmination of over a decade of preparation for flight school. My class of about fifty student pilots was split into two sections. Again, I was the one and only Black student pilot in my class. I was issued my flight suits and equipment and was assigned to ALPHA Flight for ground school and T-37 flight training. The twin jet engine T-37 was built and first flown around the time I was born in 1954. It was one of the aircraft I had read about in the *Jet Pilot* book. Ground school was all about learning the basics of flying and a lot of what I was taught was already familiar to me. One of the most important ground school lessons was to learn how to do a Parachute Landing Fall (PLF). This involved parasailing behind a truck to an altitude of about five hundred feet and then releasing ourselves to fall to the ground as if we had bailed out of an airplane. Other training was in the altitude chamber, where we experienced airsickness due to hypoxia. Hypoxia is the term given to the condition when your brain is oxygen-starved in the thin air at higher altitudes. Overall, this training was absolutely essential for pilots.

Preparation for flight training began in the simulator with sessions that covered the basics like aircraft systems, checklist procedures, aircraft limitations, emergency procedures, and learning the T-37 cockpit layout. We students had to be able to recite complex emergency procedures strictly from memory, so I spent a lot of time making sure I remembered everything I was supposed to know. There were important lessons about weather too. I was paired up with another student, Second Lieutenant Mark Stinson, and our instructor was First Lieutenant Dan. As student pilots, we had to pass all written tests with a passing grade of eighty-five or better. A student pilot couldn't fail a test more than three times. If you did, you were in trouble.

By the time we began training in the actual T-37 (affectionately known as the Tweet), we were fully aware of the intense daily pressure to study hard in order to avoid being washed out. For me, the pressure was so intense I couldn't relax or slack off much.

As I was going through this fifty-two-week flight-training program, I could definitely feel the tremendous weight of the world that only God could help me lift. A typical day of T-37 training began with a briefing on the lesson of the day. Next came a visit to the weather department to get a weather brief and flight plan filing. Then we strapped on our parachutes and headed out to the flight line to fly. I had to preflight the airplane, which included walking around the jet checking everything including the tires, oil, lights, panels, and making sure there were no fuel or hydraulic leaks. My first encounter with a T-37 crew chief reminded me of where I had come from, and I gave them the utmost respect. Stepping into that Tweet beside my flight instructor, Lieutenant Dan, was the beginning of a dream come true.

Once we completed the preflight checklists, we started the engines and taxied out to the active runway. The excitement of piloting a jet plane was the culmination of years of preparation. I completed the before-takeoff checklist and lined up on runway 13L and awaited takeoff clearance. The tower cleared us for takeoff, and I advanced those throttles to full power, also known as military power, after releasing the brakes. The Tweet's little jet engines roared to full power and we accelerated to takeoff speed. I pulled back on the yoke and we lifted off into the wild blue yonder. With landing gear up, flaps up and the after-takeoff checklist completed, I was finally on the way to fulfilling my dream of earning my silver wings, propelled by the firm determination to become a fully qualified United States Air Force pilot.

As I glanced out the windscreen during takeoff, I could see the aircraft rising above the vast Mississippi landscape below us. I climbed to altitude, and we were off to the racetrack pattern to do some landings. On what was called "outside downwind," there was a white church steeple sticking out above the trees that we used as a landmark to ensure we were on course. Lieutenant Dan asked me if I saw the steeple, and when I responded that I couldn't see it, he became upset. He took control of the aircraft and pumped the flight control stick really hard, causing my head to hit the glass canopy over the cockpit. I recall getting angry to the point of wanting to knock the hell out of him.

As I sat there steaming mad, I pondered what to do about being mistreated by the white man sitting right next to me. That's when the Holy Spirit helped me remember how my ancestors had tolerated much worse to get through some tough days. Now it was my turn. Afterward, Lieutenant Dan transferred control back to me, and we proceeded around the traffic pattern past something called the hedge row, put the flaps and landing gear out, turned base to final, lined up with the runway, and landed. Lieutenant Dan was on the controls with me as I made my very first landing. That first landing wasn't bad, and I felt great despite having a flight instructor who was referred to as a "screamer."

My first formation flight in the T-37 Tweet

I suspect that Lieutenant Dan must have been unhappy being what was called a T-37 FAIP or first-assignment instructor pilot. There was nothing glamorous about finishing UPT and being selected to be a T-37 flight instructor. We proceeded to do multiple touch-and-go landings until I got the hang of consistently landing the Tweet. Thanks to the experience gained on C-7 training flights, I remembered to use the aim-point-and-airspeed technique I heard Major Holden teach. One day I was in the vehicle that took us out to the flight line when I recognized a pilot in the vehicle who was further along in-flight training. It was Dean Martin's son, known as Dean Martin Jr. Dean Martin was a famous entertainer and actor from the '50s and '60s. His son looked just like him, and he eventually went on to become an F-4 Phantom pilot in the California Air National Guard. Unfortunately for him and his backseat pilot, they were tragically killed during a formation flight when they flew into clouds, got separated from their flight leader, and smashed into a huge mountain near Los Angeles. That's why it was crucial to pay attention to details in order to survive to fly again.

Each flight lasted around one and a half hours, and sometimes we flew two sorties, or flights, in a day. In the meantime, my supervisor approached me to inform me that I had to move off base because I was getting housing allowance. I found a decent mobile home in a trailer park near the base. It was great to have a quiet place to live while I studied for hours before and after flying. Other training flights involved flying out to a designated training area to practice maneuvers, or to the auxiliary airfield to practice landings. Area maneuvers included steep turns, stalls, spins, loops, rolls, chandelles, split Ss, barrel rolls, and other acrobatics. Each maneuver required a certain airspeed and something called energy management. One of my classmates got vertigo and another couldn't stomach flying upside down. Those guys were eventually washed out due to the inability of their bodies to handle flying at all kinds of attitudes. Thank God I didn't have any issues handling the stresses of flying.

Student pilots were often urged to do something called chair flying. That's when you literally sit in a chair and pretend to fly. While it can be hard to motivate yourself to sit in a chair and pretend to be flying, it's the best thing a student pilot could do. Why? Because when you get in a real airplane and do certain maneuvers or landings for the first time, it's as if you have already done it before. Luckily for me, I had built what looked like an airplane in my backyard during childhood and instinctively knew how to practice flying.

The most amazing thing I ever had to do in T-37 flight training was purposely stalling a T-37 at about twenty thousand feet. This involved pulling the throttles to idle and slowly raising the nose to maintain altitude until the aircraft couldn't fly anymore. As the airspeed became too slow, the airplane started to vibrate and roll off to one side and go into a diving spin. All I could see was the ground rapidly spinning around and around and around. The emergency spin recovery required six sequential steps that had to be expertly performed in perfect order, or the aircraft would continue to spin all the way into the ground and crash. Fortunately for me, my spin-recovery performance was excellent, and my instructors were very impressed.

My only emergency occurred on takeoff as I advanced the throttles for takeoff. As the T-37 barreled down the runway toward the sixty-five-knot takeoff speed, the aircraft started to veer off to the left. Ole Lieutenant Dan started screaming, "Get it back on centerline!" to which I yelled, "I can't!" He immediately grabbed control of the aircraft and applied right rudder to correct back to centerline. That was when he realized it wasn't my fault and something was terribly wrong with the aircraft. Instinctively, Lieutenant Dan slammed the throttles to idle, applied differential braking to steer back toward centerline, and notified the tower that we were aborting. That day, we came close to running off the side of the runway into the grass, and who knows how that would have ended. Ole Lieutenant Dan was huffing and puffing after that ordeal. After he gathered his composure, he somehow got the aircraft off the runway and taxied to a stop, set the brakes, and shut it down. Maintenance towed the aircraft away as we headed to debrief.

I learned another important lesson that day: Always be ready for anything, and be ready to abort if something goes wrong. Every phase of flight was carefully graded, and any unsatisfactory item was worked on until it was satisfactory. The T-37 traveled around the traffic pattern at two hundred knots and landed at around one hundred knots. I had to pass three check rides during this phase of flight school: basic flight maneuvers, acrobatics, and instrument evaluations. There was one particular flight with another flight instructor by the name of Major Guy Sumpter where I was too slow and unable to stay on top of all the procedures. In the debriefing, Major Sumpter facetiously said, "If we had crashed, you wouldn't have gotten hurt because you were so far behind the aircraft!" He was an excellent instructor, and his humor put me at ease and allowed me to once again redouble my efforts to stay ahead of the aircraft. Eventually, after flying several flights with Major Sumpter, he admitted that I had good hands when it came to flying.

After several other flights, I had a pre-solo flight to demonstrate that I could make three good landings in a row. After that third landing, Lieutenant Dan had me taxi the T-37 onto the taxiway and stop to let him out. I came to a stop, set the brakes, he got out of the aircraft, and I closed the canopy to taxi out for my first solo flight. I felt a little lonely, and it reminded me of the first time I drove a car by myself. With my childhood motto of "THE JET WILL FLY" firmly in mind, I sprouted my black wings that day and roared aloft into yonder blue skies, overcoming the weight of this world all by myself. As my poem "Black Wings" says, I got in the air and did what I love: fly like a black bird or an eagle or a mighty dove. I made several solo landings, which thankfully pleased my flight instructor, and we moved on to the next phase of my training.

On my first formation flight, my instructor gave me the controls as we flew as the lead aircraft in a two-ship formation. We had briefed what was called a pitchout and rejoin. As I went to pitch out to the right, the joystick wouldn't budge. I glanced over at my instructor, and he motioned for me to roll to the left away from the other aircraft instead of to the right toward our wingmen. At that instant I felt so terrible that I didn't have enough damn sense to know better. Apparently, T-37 instructors had been taught to brace their leg against the flight control joystick to keep a student from pitching in the wrong direction. Needless to say, I was deeply humbled and resolved to do what my OTS instructor had drilled into us, which was: PAY ATTENTION TO DETAIL!

On one of my last solo flights, I was in my practice area and decided to do a loop. As I advanced the throttles to increase the airspeed, I pulled the nose straight up, and instead of tensing my lower body, I must have held my breath. The aircraft went vertical and as it continued into inverted flight at the top of the loop, I began to lose consciousness. For a moment I was nearly out, and when I realized what was happening, I gang-loaded my oxygen regulator to 100 percent as I was trained, which allowed me to fully recover. The aircraft was inverted upside down with dangerously low airspeed and was barely flying. I quickly pushed the throttles up for more power and struggled to get the nose down to gain flying airspeed. With the nose down and those little jet engines slowly spooling up, I rolled the aircraft upright and began to do what was called border patrol. Border patrol involves flying straight and level from one side of the practice area to the other. That's what a pilot who scares the hell out of himself while solo does to calm down until it's time to head back to base and land.

On another solo flight, a fuel gauge malfunction caused me to become unsure of how much fuel I had left in the aircraft. This time I declared a precautionary status to air traffic control and headed back to base, where I landed safely. On another flight during an out-and-back flight from Columbus AFB to Fort Campbell in Kentucky, a thunderstorm gust came up and my instructor decided to cancel our flight and wait until the next day. His decision gave me a deep appreciation for the judgment a pilot must have when it comes to hazardous weather conditions. Every pilot has to know when it's unsafe to fly or risk suffering the consequences.

There was also the cross-country flight where my family members got to see me fly into Dobbins AFB in Marietta, Georgia. When we landed, the left thrust attenuator failed to open, and we had to wait for a maintenance team to come from our base and fix the problem. This process took several days, and I was able to be at home with my wife and son Jay, which was a nice treat. At three years old, Jay was really into me being an Air Force pilot, and for a moment I thought he may want to be one, too, someday.

I also had to learn how to fly in what's called instrument conditions, which is when clouds and overcast skies prevent flying under visual rules. In order to get a variety of flying instrument approaches at different airfields, I recall once having to do instrument approaches at Tuscaloosa Airport, where I performed instrument procedures flawlessly. After successfully completing all requirements in the T-37 program, I was cleared to transition to T-38 Talon training in September of 1981. Now, it was time to move on to T-38 ground school and get ready to fly the "White Rocket."

Strapped in and ready to fly the legendary T-38 Talon

Once we had been adequately prepared to fly the White Rocket, I looked forward to getting in and blasting off. The T-38 Talons I flew in training were sleek military training jets painted white with thin honeycomb wings, and had first been introduced into service in the early '60s. Normally, the student pilot sits in the front seat while the instructor sits slightly higher in the back seat. I had become familiar with the systems and everything else about this jet when I finished Air Force technical school in the fall of 1972. My experience working on the T-38 put me at a distinct advantage because no one else in my pilot training class had been a crew chief like me. Reflecting on memories of being assigned to the wash rack where I washed T-38s, it suddenly dawned on me that I was probably one of a few people who would get to wash a T-38 and fly one. Trust me, flying a T-38 is much, much better than working on it or washing it.

My class learned about the cockpit layout, systems, limitations, and emergency procedures applicable to the T-38 in ground school. An added piece of equipment needed to fly the super-fast T-38 was a G-suit, which is meant to keep a pilot from passing out like I almost did in the T-37. The jet also has an afterburner, which is needed to get that twelve-thousand-pound jet airborne. There was a red, yellow, and green indicator that sat on the glareshield in front of the pilot. The objective of this device was to keep the indicator in the green when landing and preventing students from killing themselves. You never wanted to see that indicator in the red.

My first orientation flight, called the Dollar Ride, in the T-38 was with Captain Fox, who was the flight commander. We briefed the flight, strolled out to the jet, and completed the necessary preflight checks and started the jet. Captain Fox taxied out to the runway, lit the afterburners, and we were off into the wild blue yonder. As he released the brakes while advancing the throttles to military power, we looked at the gauges to verify increased fuel flow, proper exhaust gas temperature (EGT), 100 percent rpm, and afterburner engagement. Afterburners produce a kick-in-the-pants like boost, and at the thousand-foot marker, we had to be traveling at a speed in excess of 100 kts and accelerating toward 165 kts.

In no time we had lifted off, retracted the gear and flaps, climbed to thirty thousand feet, and arrived at the practice area, where he prepared to demonstrate a few aggressive maneuvers. He rolled the T-38 upside down and applied negative Gs, which left me hanging by my straps. Now I suppose he was trying to make me puke or scare me, but I wasn't fazed at all. I said, "That was fun! Let's do it again!" Then he demonstrated several rapid aileron rolls and a loop. The T-38 needs ten thousand feet to do a loop, so he started at twenty thousand and topped out at about thirty before pulling the nose through to come down on the backside. When he realized I had the stomach for this high-performance machine, he demonstrated a few other maneuvers and then let me take the controls and get familiar with the jet. The T-38 was light on the controls, extremely maneuverable, and an awesome machine to fly.

After the air work in the practice area, we headed back to base to do some touch-and-go landings. We entered the flight traffic pattern flying 300 kts down to the end of runway 13R, where Captain Fox rolled right into a tight 60-degree bank turn. Around the 180-degree turn, he bled off airspeed to about 220 kts and started putting out flaps. With flaps out and airspeed reduced to final turn speed of about 200 kts, he rolled out on final, keeping the indicator in the green. As the T-38 comes around the descending final turn toward the runway, it constantly rumbles and shakes to remind you that you are very close to stall speed, which is the speed at which the aircraft will no longer fly. In other words, the margin of error is close and many pilots who get too slow on final have been killed before.

After demonstrating a landing, it was my turn. Of course, Captain Fox was on the controls with me, but my first T-38 landing was not bad. We did a few more landings and with our fuel getting low, Captain Fox had me bring the jet to a full stop on runway 13R and I taxied off the runway to return to our parking spot. After the flight, Captain Fox graded me on every phase of flight, and we debriefed every detail for about thirty minutes. Thereafter, I began to fly with my main instructor, Lieutenant Harpo.

The T-38 is an aircraft you cannot safely stall, so a pilot has to be careful not to let it get too slow in any phase of flight. This was very important as we performed various maneuvers in the practice areas to the south between Columbus AFB and Jackson, Mississippi. I'll never forget one solo T-38 flight when I was practicing loops over the Ole Miss or University of Mississippi football stadium. From an altitude of thirty thousand feet, I could clearly see the Rebel Flag on opposite ends of the field as I soared above. It's amazing how much of a grip the Jim Crow legacy has over that part of the country. Nevertheless, most people I encountered treated me with respect, for the most part.

Staying ahead of the T-38 would become crucial, because this jet cruises around the traffic pattern at 300 knots and its landing speed is around 170 knots. In essence, a T-38 pilot has to think well ahead as the jet travels five miles a minute in the traffic pattern. My main T-38 instructor was First Lieutenant Harpo, a young and somewhat peculiar white guy from Atlanta. Lieutenant Harpo had a helmet with a Rebel Flag emblem on it that associated him with the pathetic losers of the Civil War. Perhaps his helmet was meant to intimidate me, but I kept reminding myself why I was there. I was there to become an Air Force pilot, and nothing was going to stop me.

Life during pilot training was extremely demanding, and there was little time to do other things than flying and studying. When possible, I played video games at the recreation center and kept up my physical fitness routine. Of course, I was only around every other weekend because I drove six hours to College Park to be with my family on the weekends when we transitioned from early week to late week. That allowed me to stay home with my family a little longer. Some Sundays, I left the Atlanta area late and often got really sleepy along the way. That was when I happened to discover that smoking Black & Mild cigars somehow kept me awake. There were some nights when I would get back to Columbus and not remember half the trip. Over time, those darn cigars became addictive, and it would become a difficult habit to kick. I never did like letting anything control me or make me feel like I couldn't live without it, but those cigars had me hooked for a while. Needless to say, I learned an extremely valuable lesson about addiction the hard way.

There were times when my fellow classmates would hang out at the officer's club, but since I was the only Black student pilot in the class, it wasn't much fun. I did have a chance to mingle with some of the local Black folks in Columbus, mainly at a nightclub I affectionately called the "Come As You Are Club." I called it that because it appeared the locals got off from working at the farm or factory on Friday or Saturday and came to the nightclub just as they were—funky and ready to party. Late one night I accompanied two Kenyan student pilots to this nightclub, and that was something to remember because those guys were like wild party animals. They would drive recklessly and party well into the night.

I remember how the songs "Fire and Desire" by Rick James and Teena Marie and "Let's Groove" by Earth, Wind & Fire were so popular. Also, somewhere around the beginning of my T-38 phase of training, I agreed to rent a three-bedroom house off base with two Black Air Force Academy graduates. These guys were just starting as student pilots, so I was able to mentor them a little bit.

On one occasion, Lieutenant Harpo and I were cleared for takeoff, and I advanced the throttles toward military power for takeoff. A quick glance down at the afterburner gauges revealed a big problem that portended danger. As the jet barreled down the runway, my training kicked in and I swiftly aborted the takeoff and notified the tower that I was aborting. The right afterburner nozzles failed to activate, resulting in insufficient thrust for a safe takeoff.

The only other incident was during an instrument training

flight where I was in the back seat under a hood that forced me to use instruments only to navigate and fly approaches, but the instructor had to do the takeoff and landing. This time, with Lieutenant Harpo in the front seat, we barreled down the runway and took off into the clouds. Once in the clouds, I quickly noticed the airspeed roll back from 300 kts to 250 kts to 150 kts toward zero. As I mentioned before, the T-38 normally cruises through the air at 300 kts, and below that it will stall. Instinctively, I knew what the problem was and knew not to panic. Because he wasn't used to flying in the front seat, the instructor pilot forgot to turn on the pitot heat, which caused the pitot tube that measures airspeed to freeze over. I called the issue to his attention and he turned the pitot switch on, and the airspeed indicator recovered to indicate the correct speed.

After I finished my maneuvers-check ride evaluation, demonstrating that I could successfully perform acrobatics, instrument approaches, takeoffs, and landings, it was time to learn formation flying. The typical two-ship-formation ride involved taking off together with the wingman having to fixate on three places on the lead jet in order to stay three feet apart. Lieutenant Harpo demonstrated the first part of the formation flight as we blasted off. We entered the practice area and began to do pitchouts and rejoins. Again, a pitchout is a maneuver where the lead aircraft rolls into a 60-degree bank and pulls to turn 180 degrees at about 450 kts. The wingman then follows about five seconds later with a 60-degree bank turn and follows the leader and rejoins on the wing once again at three feet apart. Now this is the most nerve-racking part of formation flight. After a pitchout and rejoin, the lead aircraft would start doing acrobatics like a barrel roll that has the aircraft slowly rolling 360 degrees through the sky.

I recall being in a 90-degree bank going about 500 kts looking up or down at this T-38 that's feet away and thinking about how daring this kind of flying was. It was surreal being in that T-38 and realizing that only by the grace of God was I there. Another thrilling aspect of formation flying was close trail, where the lead aircraft flies various acrobatic patterns and the wingman tucks in slightly below the leader's tail with about three feet of separation. After seeing these maneuvers thoroughly briefed and demonstrated, I built up enough confidence and acquired the nerves of steel necessary to confidently fly in close proximity to another aircraft.

When it was my turn to take the controls, I was ultimately able to successfully fly formation almost like the infamous Air Force Thunderbird precision flight demonstration team I had first seen at Robins AFB during my youth. At first, it was hard to stay in place because I was moving the joystick too much. With some expert instruction from Lieutenant Harpo and another instructor, Captain Larry Dreaden, I was able to use minute movements of the joystick to stay in formation.

Four ship T-38 formation flight nearing UPT graduation

Captain Larry Dreaden and I had some death-defying incidents when I flew with him. Once, we lost sight of our wingman, and while trying to coordinate a rejoin, we found ourselves flying toward our wingman at four hundred knots, which Captain Dreaden finally realized was too damn dangerous. That was when he decided to terminate the formation flight and return to base. Most notably, the one and only check ride I have ever failed in my entire flying career was my formation checkout flight. The white evaluator pilot I was flying with accused me of nearly colliding with the lead jet as we were returning to base. Perhaps he got scared or didn't want me to be qualified to fly close formation. Whatever the reason, I didn't care, because it wouldn't keep me from passing the recheck and getting my wings.

On another flight, Captain Dreaden and I were making what's referred to as a base turn to final, which means turning to line up with the runway. With me flying the jet descending through a traffic pattern altitude of three thousand feet, we individually sighted another T-38 on a straight-in approach directly below us. After we both spotted the jet, below us about the same time I jammed the throttles forward to afterburner to get us up and away from the other airplane. I would estimate we came within ten feet of hitting the other T-38 below us. Nevertheless, we shook it off and continued flying around the pattern, all while counting our blessings and keeping a sharp eye out for any other airplanes.

Strangely, I never really had any real fear even when I came close to tragedy. It always felt like there was something looking out for me all throughout my flying career and throughout my entire life. The same was true in other parts of life too. In December 1981, for example, while driving through Tuscaloosa, Alabama, I was hit from behind by a driver following too closely. Thankfully, I wasn't hurt and had the ability to continue driving home with a banged-up car.

As of March 1982, it seemed as if the past fifty-two weeks had gone by like a whirlwind, and I finally could breathe a sigh of relief and take a moment to absorb it all. After completing all requirements for the UPT curriculum, we were scheduled to fly in a four-ship formation of T-38s. On this flight I took my camera and was able to take some memorable photos of our jets doing some cool maneuvers in formation. After that flight, my classmates and I prepared for graduation day and looked forward to heading to other bases to learn to fly the aircraft we had been assigned to. During the year, I learned that my unit back at Dobbins AFB would be trading in the C-7s for brand-new C-130H models built by Lockheed across the field.

Mother, Marcus, Me and Rene at UPT graduation

In the summer of 1981, my wife Thelma became pregnant with my third son. Because she was due in mid-March, her doctor ordered her not to travel. So, my three-year-old son, Johnnie III, or as we called him, Jay, rode with me back to Columbus as I readied myself for what would be the best day of my life. I was twenty-eight years old and about to achieve the greatest goal ever. On graduation day, March 18, 1982, my family members, including many nieces and nephews, were able to witness me walking across the stage and receiving my pilot wings. My mother was there to see me graduate, and I could sense she had spent a lot of time praying for me. I know it was her prayers that helped protect me throughout my flying career. I was so elated I forgot to salute Colonel Zakreski as he congratulated me on stage. He whispered, "You forgot to salute me!" which prompted me to snap to attention and give him the biggest salute of his life. Someone took a photo of my brother Kirby pinning on my shiny new wings to show that I had finally become a fully qualified Air Force pilot. Overall, it was a delightful day and it felt really good to be surrounded by a loving family.

Several days after returning home to College Park, we had a new addition to the family. In late March 1982, Marion Alexander Jones was born, which was the same day his mother was born. How cool is that? Marion is named after his mother's father, Marion Devoe. Mr. Devoe had four daughters but never had a son, so it made him proud to know his grandchild would carry his name. This time, I got to witness this child being born, and boy, was that a sight to see my youngest son come into the world!

Before I left Columbus AFB, I was required to take a flight physical exam, but I failed the eye exam for 20/20 distance vision. Much to my dismay, I was now required to wear glasses whenever I flew. All that intense reading required to pass all of my exams had nearly ruined my distant vision. On the bright side, my new glasses allowed me to see distant objects much better. Now with my new glasses, it was time to regroup and get ready to head to Little Rock AFB in Little Rock, Arkansas for the three-month-long basic and advanced C-130 qualification course. The C-130 Hercules is a large, stubby-looking high-wing versatile cargo aircraft with four turboprop engines. It was designed and first put in service around 1954, the year I was born. As of 2021, it is still being produced by the Lockheed Martin Corporation and is flown by the Air Force.

First there was ground school and then simulator sessions before beginning flights. As opposed to the one-and-a-half-hour training flights during UPT, C-130 training flights were four hours in length with two students, along with the instructor pilot, flight engineer, and loadmaster. In the span of those four hours, each student would get to do about twenty landings each thanks to the touch-and-go procedures that had us touching down and resetting the flaps and trim before adding power and taking off again. Next came C-130 airdrop school, where we learned how to plan and brief an airdrop mission.

After learning the basics, we got hands-on experience flying a timed, low-level route through the Arkansas countryside over the bridge at Lake Maumelle and making an airdrop on the drop zone (DZ) to the west of the base. The expert ability to plan and deliver men or equipment to a DZ at a precise time was a testament to the professionalism and skill of C-130 aircrews. Then came the most challenging part of C-130 flying: the assault takeoff and landings. An assault takeoff involves holding the brakes until you can push the throttles up to near max power and zipping down that short runway to leap off and climb rapidly to about 3,000 feet. The assault landing involves lowering the nose to a steep angle, focusing on a narrow airstrip from about 2,500 feet, and then aiming short of the threshold to swap ends and land successfully on that short piece of land. The objective is to plant the aircraft firmly on the ground to dissipate energy and yank the throttles into full reverse while using maximum braking to stop in about 2,000 feet.

After successfully passing all required exams and check rides, I was an official C-130 copilot with the goal of returning years later to become an aircraft commander after gaining enough experience flying in the right seat. I left Little Rock AFB to return home and served out the rest of my active-duty time until October 1982. Because my unit was yet to receive a single new C-130, I had to travel to Pope AFB in North Carolina several times to stay current on landings on the aircraft.

One exciting incident occurred back at Dobbins AFB as I was working as a landing zone (LZ) officer when the C-7 pilots were practicing short field landings on the assault strip in extremely gusty crosswinds. I actually witnessed a C-7 fly an approach to the LZ when a strong gust of wind turned that airplane ninety degrees at about a hundred feet. Those pilots quickly realized landing was not an option and they slammed the throttles full forward to maximum power and climbed out toward the main base. That was as close as I had ever come to seeing an airplane crash. It also made me redouble my efforts to always be safe and become good at landing, especially with a strong crosswind.

Building Flight Time

I RETURNED TO work at Southern Bell, where the company put me through a Sobel programming class once again. I cannot express how much I hated going back to that boring office job, but I needed the income to support my family. After about a year of being back at work at Southern Bell and only able to fly nights and occasionally weekends, I was moved to a new work section where I was the only Black person in that group. That became a setup for failure, and the job became unbearable. Without proper assistance on a complex project I was assigned, my immediate supervisor pressured me for results. Seeing the handwriting on the wall, I cleverly drafted a resignation letter and left the job in October 1983. Because of the recession and air traffic control strike, flying jobs were scarce, so I resorted to flying with the Air Force Reserves whenever they needed me.

Over the next two years I flew various missions. One particular mission was called Reserve Operational Support (ROS), which called for flying to seven or eight Air Force bases over a seven-day period carrying cargo and people. There was one ROS trip that had us scheduled to fly into Chicago O'Hare Airport, which was the busiest airport in the world at the time. Captain J. D. Bailey and I had briefed up for the approach to O'Hare, but when we were handed over to approach control, all of our plans went out the window. That air traffic controller started barking out instructions so fast we were unable to keep up. Once the controller realized we had never been to such a busy airport before, he became more helpful, but it was a wild ride for a while.

I often flew with Captain Gordon Mushtare, who was one of my favorite aircraft commanders to fly with. Gordon and I flew missions to Bermuda, Puerto Rico, Antigua, St. Croix, and other places in the Caribbean. Perhaps one of the most rewarding flying experiences was a weeklong mission with Major Skip Mason to Europe including the countries of England, Spain, Italy, and Germany. On the way back we stopped overnight at Lajes Air Base in the Azores, which is in the middle of the Atlantic Ocean.

Standing outside C-130H at Lajes in the Azores

The most demanding trip was out to Nellis AFB in Las Vegas, Nevada, where we participated in a Red Flag Exercise, which was a very realistic war game–like adventure. I was paired up with a highly experienced Vietnam War-era C-130 pilot and aircraft commander named Major Clint Tykeson. I never knew how good a C-130 pilot could be until I flew with Clint through the mountains and in the valleys of the Nevada desert, flying some fifty to a hundred feet above the ground. Clint was masterful at doing steep banked turns to evade an F-15 fighter jet that was trying get a radar lock on us to simulate shooting us down. As a matter of fact, I was so afraid we were going to crash and burn that it was hard to fully function as a copilot should. Frankly, I was forced to come to terms with the real possibility that I could die that day. Learning to accept death or die before dying was absolutely essential to learning how to live without fear. Thereafter, the paralyzing fear that had gripped me was gone. I somehow felt liberated from fear and was actually able to enjoy sitting in the copilot seat watching Clint skillfully fly that C-130 like it was a fighter jet too. Accepting death before dying would someday in the future become something that I would read about in *The New Earth* by Eckhart Tolle.

A tragic event occurred around this time when my favorite singer, Marvin Gaye, was killed by his father on April 1, 1984. Marvin's unique style, awesome voice, and magnificent music had had a profound effect on me. Even though Marvin left us with great inspirational music, I found myself mourning his death for a while. I would play his music and even read a biography about his life entitled *Divided Soul* by David Ritz. The one song that captures the essence of his life is entitled "Dream of a Lifetime." This underappreciated masterpiece of music perfectly sums up my life as well. The dream of my lifetime had been to become an Air Force pilot, and I was truly living the dream.

Another pilot, Lieutenant Mike Wooten, who had flown with me on that Europe trip, was working for a small cargo carrier out of Fulton County Airport. He convinced me to fly with him in a Merlin Metroliner, an airplane with loud twin turboprop engines. That cold winter night, we flew a trip down to Tallahassee and Orlando, and back to Atlanta. We had to load the airplane, fly it in the middle of the night, and unload it at each stop.

After returning from that trip the next morning, I firmly decided flying night cargo was definitely not for me. I resorted to continuing to build flight time with my Air Force Reserve unit by flying four-hour local flights, multiple rotations to Panama in Central America, and some weekend trips to places like MacDill AFB in Tampa. Rotations to Panama were missions based out to Howard Air Base in Panama, where we flew to Honduras, El Salvador, Colombia, Costa Rica, Peru, Bolivia, Chile, Paraguay, Argentina, and Uruguay. Of course, I got the chance to learn Spanish while down there. Flying in that mountainous region was so dangerous that the Air Force wisely limited the flying to daytime only. Unfortunately, far too many Air Force aircraft had previously smashed into mountains down there. Luckily, I flew with Major Chuck Burch, who was another highly experienced C-130 pilot who had flown in Vietnam. Major Burch and I had different personalities and dispositions, but I learned a lot from this hardnosed, combat-hardened pilot.

A memorable mission was to La Paz in Bolivia, which is thirteen thousand feet above sea level with a twenty-two-thousand-foot mountain range nearby. Landing there was interesting because the air was so thin the airplane performance was diminished. After spending the night there in that thin atmosphere, we departed the city to fly back to Panama. We rolled and rolled and rolled down that thirteen-thousand-foot runway and couldn't get enough flying airspeed until near the end of the runway. Then we had to slowly climb in a circular patter to gain enough altitude to get over that nearby 22,000 ft mountain range. The flying in Central and South America we did during the Reagan administration would come to be associated with some shady activities the American government was involved in. Nevertheless, I was never shot at—as far as I know.

Airdrop missions were exciting too. My unit would often be tasked to drop Army paratroopers in paratrooper school at Fort Benning in Columbus, Georgia. We would fly down there and load up with ninety paratroopers at a time, take them out to the Friar Drop Zone (DZ), drop them, and return to the airfield every twenty minutes to load up and do it again and again. Overall, logging time in the C-130 was great for building flight time. Soon I was promoted to first lieutenant, and then to captain.

Flying right co-pilot on the C-130H

Occasionally, I would fly in the left seat with an instructor pilot in the right seat so I could get experience being an aircraft commander. Once, I was on an interesting trip to Washington State.

We had been tasked to fly a two-ship mission from McChord Air Force Base to a drop zone in Yakama, which was to the east of the base. Our low-level route took us through some of the deepest valleys I have ever seen. As I flew along the valley floor sitting in the left seat, I recall following the lead C-130, which was about two thousand feet ahead of us. Every now and then there would be a house nestled in the hillside, and as we flew by you could actually look up at some of the houses. That was how low we were flying.

All of a sudden, the lead aircraft came upon a steep mountain ridge and rapidly climbed to crest the ridge ahead. As I began to apply power to climb over the same ridgeline, it started to seem like the aircraft climb rate would be insufficient to get over the mountain ahead of us. That was when I instinctively applied maximum power on all four-turboprop engines as I gently pulled the nose up while I maintained a safe flying airspeed. I knew I couldn't pull back too far because if the aircraft got below stall speed, we would crash and burn.

With our hearts pounding, we just barely made it over that ridge and everyone on my crew felt blessed when God once again saved the day. Thereafter, we wisely abandoned flying in formation through valleys and over the hills, and essentially operated as single-ship flights. It was the safest thing to do, and we all lived to tell about it. These are the kinds of unforgettable, death-defying experiences that no amount of training can provide.

Over time, I developed a serious interest in becoming an airline pilot since many of the pilots in my unit also flew for Delta, American, Eastern, or Piedmont Airlines. They told me about the ability to earn a lot of money while working about fifteen days a month. So, when I learned that United Airlines was hiring, I began applying for airline jobs. In March of 1985, I interviewed with United Airlines and a few weeks later got a rejection letter in the mail. Shortly thereafter, the pilot's union at United Airlines called a strike that lasted about thirty days. Unbeknownst to me, United Airlines had a long history of discriminating against Black pilots. In fact, there was only a small number of Black pilots at any commercial airline due to entrenched racial bias against Black people. Thankfully, Congresswoman Cardiss Collins and Congressman John Conyers were instrumental in bringing attention to the lack of diversity and inclusion for Blacks at the airlines. The EEOC was also investigating racial bias in airline hiring.

Once I had enough flight time, I was able to get hired at an up-and-coming little regional airline called Atlantic Southeast Airlines (ASA) in January 1986. The memory of this period corresponds to the tragic in-flight explosion of the *Challenger* space shuttle. Thanks to Lieutenant Mike Wooten and another pilot in my unit, Captain Bill "Jet" Jackson, I was able to start my illustrious career as a commercial airline pilot. Getting hired at ASA was a part of my new plan to get hired as a pilot at Delta Airlines. ASA was a feeder airline for Delta and soon became partially owned by Delta. I was hired at ASA as a Shorts 360 copilot based out of Atlanta's Hartsfield-Jackson Airport (ATL).

My ground school training included the unique experience of visiting the Atlanta Air Traffic Control Center in Hampton, Georgia and the Atlanta Airport Tower. There I got to see how air traffic controllers skillfully guide airplanes in the southeast region and in and out of what would become the busiest airport in the world. The Shorts 360 was a boxlike twin-engine turboprop airplane that carried about twenty-eight passengers, depending on the outside temperature and baggage load. My Shorts 360 flight training began with my instructor and I traveling from Atlanta as passengers on the last flight to Asheville, North Carolina. Once there, we would take the same airplane we had just flown in on and fly it down to Greenville Airport in South Carolina and train in the middle of the night. Honestly, my training in the actual airplane was very good for a commuter airline.

The most memorable training event was on a night flight when my flight instructor pulled one throttle back on takeoff to simulate an engine failure right at liftoff. As we climbed out, I had just completed the appropriate emergency procedures to simulate shutting down the engine when he pulled back the other engine to simulate a dual engine failure. Then he said, "What are you going to do now?"

I replied, "Land straight ahead with wings level." That was what we had been taught in ground school.

He then said, "There's a runway behind you, right?" to which I replied, "Yes!" He said, "Well, turn around and land on it!"

Amazingly, I was able to keep enough flying airspeed and turn the aircraft around 180 degrees and glide to a power-off landing. This clever bit of instruction gave me a lot of confidence in this somewhat ugly airplane. Once I finished training, I went on to fly numerous regional flights in and out of ATL to places like Macon, Huntsville, Asheville, Columbus, Greenville, Dothan, Montgomery, Augusta, and Valdosta.

Next came the beneficial opportunity to head back to Little Rock AFB to attend the C-130 Aircraft Commander Upgrade Course in 1987. Since no one in my unit actively pushed young copilots like me to return to Little Rock AFB to upgrade to aircraft commander, I submitted my own paperwork for consideration. When I asked the managers at ASA for a leave of absence, they said no. Fortunately, I knew there was a federal law that prevented employers from keeping military reservists from attending training events or serving on temporary active-duty assignments. I sent a well-written letter to ASA management, and they promptly granted my three-month leave of absence. I drove my copper-colored Toyota Corolla SR5 out to Little Rock AFB and began training. While there, I was able to reconnect with a long-lost high school classmate, Willie Bronner. Willie was a fun-loving dude that I always enjoyed hanging out with, and we made the best of our time together. His brother, Lieutenant Colonel Johnny Bronner, was a C-130 navigator and we got to fly together on an airdrop mission. Both Bronner brothers from Americus were great guys to hang out with. A lot of the training was the same as before, only this time I was training to be the man in charge in the left seat.

Luckily for me, I still had my ASA crew badge, so I was able to ride the jump seat on a new Black-owned airline based out of Atlanta called Air Atlanta. Air Atlanta was founded in 1984 by a very ambitious young Black entrepreneur and Dartmouth College graduate named Michael Hollis. I would periodically leave C-130 training and drive from Little Rock to Memphis and fly on the jump seat on Air Atlanta to and from Atlanta. Air Atlanta crews, who were mostly former Eastern Airlines crewmembers, flew Boeing 727 jets outfitted with all first-class seats, and the service was absolutely phenomenal. It's too bad the airline was ultimately forced out of business later that same year in 1987, probably due to a lack of capital funding, hostile competitive forces, and racial bias.

Once my training was completed, I drove back home to College Park to return to ASA and serve with my reserve unit as a new fully qualified C-130 aircraft commander. During the ensuing years, my marriage to Thelma became rocky and unstable. It became apparent in earlier years that we had started to drift apart as I traveled more, and she was left to raise our sons. One of the sad consequences of being a pilot was an unbalanced family life because of my extensive time away from home. As I stated before, things go haywire when life is not in balance, and my life was definitely unbalanced during these times. Nevertheless, it takes courage to face the difficulties of life head on.

Around this time, the Dobbins AFB newspaper called the *Minuteman* published a story about me for Black History Month. It turns out that from 1982 until 1993, I was the first and only Black C-130 pilot in my unit, the 700th Tactical Airlift Squadron. This was a time when those in control of a company or government agency would try to find one Black person to give the appearance of diversity and inclusion. Another name for this practice is called "tokenism." It didn't matter to Black people like me, because many of us who were the first or token to integrate a previously all-white group would eventually advocate for other Blacks to come on board.

With the same determination I had to become an Air Force pilot, I was determined to fulfill my new dream of becoming a Delta

Airlines pilot. I didn't really want to fly for any other airline, because Delta was my hometown airline and the perfect airline for me—at least, so I thought. My distant eyesight had been diminished from having to study so much in UPT, so I had to do eye exercises every day to get my eyes back to 20/20, a requirement to get hired at Delta. John Bailey, who was a Delta pilot, did what he could to get me an interview. My fellow church member and Delta executive John Cox put in a good word for me as well. I listed Delta Black pilots John Bailey and Chris Franks on my application along with several other white pilots who were still in my Air Force Reserve unit.

Rumors were going around about what to expect from a Delta interview. One thing to anticipate was a probing interview by the company psychiatrist, the personnel manager, and a retired captain. While the interview seemed to go well with the psychiatrist, the personnel manager asked me some unusually personal questions dealing with my family. Furthermore, the retired captain I interviewed with engaged in an awkward conversation that really disturbed me and left me puzzled. I didn't know whether he was trying to piss me off or what. Nevertheless, I tried to do my level best to be cordial and pass the interview so I could get hired. In the end, I left that interview totally bewildered but still optimistic.

During 1987, I desperately tried to keep every aspect of my life in balance. A lot of my off time was spent trying to stay in shape and spend time with my family, especially my sons. I would bring my oldest son, Curtis, to our home so he could get to know his younger brothers. I wanted to make going to church a family affair, as I wanted my sons to have a strong religious foundation.

While religion was important to me, I was beginning to probe much deeper into Christianity. Even still, I had a whole lot of curiosity about the mysterious origins of religion and a burning desire to get a better understanding about Jesus Christ and the role of the church. For some reason, I just couldn't blindly accept everything I was told about religion at face value. There seemed to be much more to learn about a religion that impacts and influences (or, more accurately, controls) so many lives. Ultimately, I would come to interpret religion much differently than most people. The 2016 movie *Birth of a Nation* starring Nate Parker is one such film that clearly revealed how religion was cleverly used by white people to keep enslaved Black people in check. This is why my curiosity about religion led me to question everything I had read or been told.

I also spent time with my sons playing catch on the front lawn and playing video games. I would often jog through our neighborhood, and one day my nine-year-old son Jay wanted to come along. So, Jay and I set off jogging through the neighborhood, and he could barely keep up. After about a mile of jogging Jay started to turn red as he was huffing and puffing. While I was impressed with his desire to keep up with me, I eventually had to stop and walk with him the rest of the way.

Of all my three sons, Jay was the most active and energetic. At first, I sensed that he wanted to be a pilot, too, but that budding ambition soon faded. My youngest son, Marion, whom we called Al, was now five years old, and he and Jay kept us busy. Marion would also have an interest in becoming a pilot, too, but health issues interfered with his desires. Curtis, my oldest son, was being raised by his mom, Jo Anne, in Northwest Atlanta and I tried to get all three of them together as often as I could. My goal was to take them on a vacation at least once a year. Once, I took them to Panama City, Florida, and on another occasion, I took them to Los Angeles, California, where we spent time with my savior, Alvin Bowen.

One day, I went outside to check the mailbox and there was a letter from Delta Airlines. Could this be the day I got notice of a start date at Delta? No way! Delta had sent me their standard rejection letter, and I was absolutely devastated. Getting rejected by Delta was like a swift kick in the gut. Even though I had been bewildered by the interview, I was still hopeful about getting hired by Delta and flying out of Atlanta's airport. I actually believe I was in grieving for quite a while. The last thing I wanted to do was work for another airline and be based in another city, which would require me to commute throughout my entire career. On the other hand, I had also reapplied to United Airlines because they had reached out to me to urge me to apply once again.

Little did I know, the EEOC had forced United to agree to hire more Black pilots, so they were scrambling to find any Black pilot who was thoroughly qualified. Soon, I had notification from

United that I was accepted and was put in a pool of applicants to be hired the next year in June 1988. Meanwhile, I was still flying with ASA and the Air Force Reserves.

From ASA to United's Friendly Skies

IN 1987, MY life was about to change in some dramatic ways. I had transitioned to the De Havilland Dash 7 airplane, a high-wing four-engine turboprop airliner that could take off and land in short distances. Usually, pilots only fly one type of aircraft at a time. Nevertheless, for about a year, I was flying one four-engine turboprop airplane for the military and another for the airline. This was not an easy time, because I had to be proficient on both types of airplanes. Naturally, I had the weight of the world on my shoulders, and once again life was getting out of balance on the home front. Even though we were still together, my marriage to Thelma was rocky and wasn't getting any better. We sought marriage counseling, but that didn't seem to help.

At ASA, I had put in for and got a Brasilia EMB 120 twin-engine turboprop captain bid. Now I had a serious choice to make. Stay at ASA as a Brasilia captain in Atlanta or take the job at United starting out as a Boeing 727 flight engineer in Chicago. The Boeing 727 was a three-engine turbojet airliner that required three flight deck crewmembers, a pilot, copilot, and a flight engineer who sat sideways behind the pilots at a complex panel full of gauges and switches. The flight engineer was an entry-level position responsible for managing the fuel, hydraulic, pneumatic, pressurization, and air conditioning systems. Realistically, the decision wasn't that hard, because working conditions at ASA were contentious and I couldn't see myself working there for another thirty years.

I left ASA for United Airlines and began training at the Denver Flight Training Center on June 27, 1988. United didn't pay for a place to live during the two months of training, so I, like many other newly hired pilots, stayed at a cheap, dumpy old hotel near the training center. That old hotel was named the Ski and Swim, but we newly hired pilots gave it a new name. We called it the Sink and Swim. The training was fairly easy due to my having completed a home 727 flight engineer course that helped me get a grasp of the systems and procedures.

After completing training in August, I had my family fly out to spend some time in the Denver area. Prior to leaving, I wanted to take them up into the mountains, so I rented a car at the airport. I drove them through the foothills of the Rocky Mountains with the goal of driving to the top of Mt. Evans, a fourteen-thousand-foot mountain. Being short on time, I stopped short of the mountaintop at about thirteen thousand feet, where I let the kids roam around. Soon they were gasping for air, because above ten thousand feet the air is so thin you cannot breathe normally. That was a little science lesson for them to remember. Thereafter, we returned to the Denver airport and flew home to Atlanta through Chicago.

For the next several years, I would commute to Chicago to sit on call on reserve awaiting flying assignments. I ended up flying as a flight engineer of many flights throughout the United States. At the nine-month point, I had to take a probationary check ride or evaluation on a flight from Cleveland, Ohio (CLE) to Denver, Colorado (DEN) with a white Denver-based captain I had never met. I deadheaded; in other words, I flew as a passenger to Cleveland and went down to the flight operations office to meet the captain by the name of Ralph Stewart. As I approached the captain and introduced myself, he blurted out, "Don't we hire white pilots anymore?" He wouldn't even shake my hand! I was absolutely stunned!

I replied, "I think so," and feeling dejected, I promptly headed to the aircraft to do my preflight inspection and setup with my evaluator.

After takeoff and while cruising in flight to Denver, the other flight deck crew members were engaged in a conversation about football, the Denver Broncos in particular. Captain Stewart remarked that he and the Broncos coach, Dan Reeves, were from the same hometown. At that point I perked up and said he's from my hometown too!

Ole Captain Stewart turned around toward me and said, "You from Americus, Georgia, too?"

I said, "Yes, I am," and his whole attitude toward me changed for the better in an instant.

Thereafter he asked me if I knew Jim Long, who had been a childhood neighbor. Jim was a Black man who worked for years at the restaurant owned by Captain Stewart's dad in Americus. I told him I knew him well. The copilot and my evaluator on the flight deck that day had no idea that during my childhood days Black people weren't allowed to eat in Stewart's Restaurant because of Jim

Crow laws. All in all, Captain Stewart gained a brand-new appreciation for me, although he never even thought about apologizing for insulting comments back at the Cleveland Airport. It really didn't matter to me, because I never expected to be openly welcomed by white pilots, who often assumed that lesser-qualified Black pilots were taking jobs from white pilots. Subconsciously, I had always known that in reality the white American power structure had never originally intended for Black people to be free, educated, treated equally, or allowed to vote. That's the reason racism will likely always remain a major problem and an unnecessary burden in this country.

On June 19, 1989, a United Airlines DC-10 airliner with three jet engines was carrying 296 people on board and flying over the state of Iowa when the number-two engine came apart, seriously damaging the flight controls. I knew two of the people on board: flight attendant Donna McGrady and pilot Peter Allen, whom I had flown with at ASA. Here again a lesson about being out of balance came from this aircraft that crash-landed at the Sioux City, Iowa, airport that day. A defective part in the number-two engine mounted on the tail broke apart and slung hot metal that severed critical hydraulic lines. The crew struggled to control the aircraft and did their best to land safely. Nevertheless, they lost control near the runway and the aircraft crashed and rolled into a fireball. Fortunately, parts of the aircraft stayed intact and the two people I knew that were on board survived without serious injury. In fact, the majority of people on board survived.

Thereafter, the number 232 seemed to haunt me by mysteriously appearing before me periodically on car tag numbers, hotel room numbers, addresses, and numerous other places. At first it was somewhat scary because of the strange and eerie association with a deadly plane crash. On other occasions, I would hear someone say

232 as well. Before long, I definitely knew it couldn't be a coincidence. Perhaps God was trying to show me or tell me something, but I have never really been able to figure out what. Coincidentally, at some point I read about the United 232 crash in a book that led me to watch the movie *Field of Dreams*, which came out in May 1989. What's the connection? United 232 had crash-landed in an Iowa cornfield. The field of dreams in the movie had been constructed in the middle of an Iowa cornfield.

As I watched the movie alone at my home around 1993, the story of a grown man reconnecting with his dead father resonated with me. Actually, I became very emotional, and cried when Kevin Costner's character connected with his deceased dad in that movie. Thereafter, I often wondered if my father, whom I have no recollection of, was somehow communicating with me in an odd way through the number 232. Maybe, someday, the exact meaning of seeing or hearing 232 so often will be revealed to me. Until then, I will just embrace 232 as a spiritual sign instead of the fear that used to come with it. Overall, I just have to be patient and wait until this monumental mystery is revealed to me.

This mysterious chain of events and some other strange things happened around the time my marriage to Thelma was unraveling. At the very least, I learned that being in a rocky marriage is a clear indication your life is out of balance. We had some contentious disagreements, and it became apparent a divorce was the only viable solution. Nevertheless, I am eternally grateful to Thelma for loving me and birthing and raising my two younger sons, Johnnie and Marion. Personally, I was ill equipped to overcome the overwhelming challenges that come with marriage.

Before Thelma and I parted ways, I did muster enough courage to go to my pastor, the Rev. Sargent, seeking guidance. I also asked him how to read and comprehend the Bible. I wanted to somehow get closer to God and find redemption. His advice to me was to use divine guidance on where to start reading the Bible. Nevertheless, the Bible is a historic and sacred book that has a lot of wisdom, but I never could find anything that gave me the clear guidance I needed. Ironically, our church was on the verge of a split, so I sought out a new church where I could find a spiritual connection. The random act of reading the Bible gave me some hope, but I desperately needed so much more from Christianity. Once again, I was prompted to probe deeper into the history and origins of religion, hoping to understand how to find peace of mind.

I clearly remember sitting on the steps in our home telling my eight-year-old and twelve-year-old sons that I wouldn't be living with them anymore. Deep down, I could tell they were saddened. We eventually split up and I went to live in an apartment nearby, and ultimately moved across town to Dekalb County in 1992. At one point, I lost just about everything I owned and was nearly broke. Getting through each day was a struggle, but thankfully, good music helped me endure it all. By the end of 1991, our divorce papers were final. Recognizing the finality of our marriage, I was suddenly overcome with emotion, and broke down and cried like a baby. After trying to figure out why I had that emotional breakdown, it finally occurred to me one day that this was the very first time I had become a complete failure at anything meaningful I was involved in. I had failed to live up to the expectations set forth by my chosen religion and the marriage vows we had taken over ten years ago.

This failure was a major personal blow to my self-esteem. Nevertheless, I was free again. I was once again left searching for that one perfect woman who would stay in my corner, as the song says. By the grace of God, I began trying to figure out how to rebuild my life and get it back in balance. Reflecting on this dreadful time, it is apparent that I was subconsciously sabotaging my health and never realized it. Never before had I been at such a low point in my life. It seemed like all of my sins had caught up with me and I was deeply burdened with having to start all over again with virtually nothing. Unbeknownst to me, the guilt I carried from committing so-called "sins" was causing me to self-destruct. Therefore, in order to save myself, I had to learn more about religion and how to deal with what I refer to as the illusion of sin. Ordinarily, a person in my predicament would be wise to seek professional counseling, but because of my position as an airline pilot, it really wasn't a viable option, as any pilot who seeks mental health counseling is subject to being grounded.

I searched for viable alternatives so I could continue to earn a living. I instinctively started reading a whole lot of self-help books, which helped me immensely. One of the first self-help books I read was *The Road Less Traveled* by M. Scott Peck. In the very first sentence he says, "Life is difficult." This is when I started to understand how to find the balance I needed to overcome the weight of the world and its problems. Thank God I had enough sense to seek wisdom beyond the Bible and religion, or else I may never have found my way. One important thing I learned to do is forgive grudges by embracing the "Let go and let God" philosophy. Thankfully, this helped to alleviate some of my guilt about failing at marriage and released me to seek forgiveness for my shortcomings. Soon, I began to recover and thrive again.

For the first time in my life, I became serious about studying human nature, persuasion, influence, religion, and spirituality. There were also some people I met along the way who helped me get through some dark and difficult days. I shall always be deeply indebted to some very special people and another "sweet thing" who stuck by me and gave me the love and affection I sorely needed. In 1992, I went back to the United Airlines training center to attend DC-10 flight engineer school, the same type of airplane that operated as United 232 which had crashed in Sioux City a few years earlier. I took the bid on this airplane to challenge my fears and make more money so I could fly desirable trips between Chicago and Honolulu, Hawaii.

Standing in front of the DC-10 in Orlando

My time on the DC-10 was even more eventful, especially when I flew several trips with Captain J. B. Captain J. B. was what they call a line check airman on the DC-10. He was also referred to as a scab because he didn't go on strike with all the other pilots at United Airlines in 1985. On one particular early-morning flight from Chicago to a snowy Denver Airport with overcast skies, Captain J. B. was giving flight instruction to new First Officer

Wendy Morse and he let her fly the aircraft until we broke out of the clouds at about three hundred feet. Because the Denver Airport runways were all snow-covered, he couldn't let her land due to restrictions on new pilots landing on snow-covered runways.

So, Captain J. B. took the controls and landed on what was an extremely slick and icy runway. From my flight engineer seat behind the pilots, I could tell the runway was very slippery. As Captain J. B. applied brakes, the aircraft anti-skid system immediately kicked in periodically releasing the brakes, which was supposed to keep the aircraft from skidding. Because the runway was deemed contaminated with snow and ice underneath, Captain J. B. only used the number-two engine for reverse, and he left the two wing engines at idle. As we were about three quarters down the runway and slowed to about five knots, the Denver tower controller asked us to expedite to the end. First Officer Wendy Morse acknowledged the tower controller's request and Captain J. B. pushed the throttles up to hurry to the end.

I imagine the aircraft speed got up to around twenty knots, and as we approached the turnoff point at the runway's end, he began to use that number-two or tail-mounted engine in reverse and brakes to slow enough to make the ninety-degree turn. As he firmly applied the brakes, that three-hundred-thousand-pound DC-10 started sliding toward snowplow tractors at the end of the runway getting ready to plow the snow once we cleared the runway. From my point of view, the snowplows disappeared below the nose as we closed in on them. Captain J. B. instinctively stood on the brakes while holding on to that number-two reverser lever with a death grip in the full reverse position. I saw the yellow snowplows reappear in the windscreen, backing up at full speed to get out of harm's way. That runway was slicker than snot that morning, and that big jet didn't seem to slow down at all. And that was when Captain J. B. blurted out, "OH SH—!"

While Wendy watched in horror, I realized Captain J. B. was completely out of ideas and needed help quickly. This highly experienced airline captain was utterly frozen and scared stiff. In what seemed like a miracle from God, everything slowed down into milliseconds, allowing me the time to ask myself, "What can stop this big airplane on this *slick-ass runway?* The answer came to me in an instant. *Reverse thrust on the two wing engines!"*

Recognizing that I was in no position from the flight engineer seat to activate the other reversers, I loudly yelled out to First Officer Morse, "He needs more reverse!" Fortunately, she had enough sense and awareness to grab the other two reversers and pull them up into the reverse thrust position.

That huge DC-10 started rumbling and shaking as we gradually slowed to a stop. That was when ole Captain J. B. came to his senses, mumbling something about get them out. We didn't know whether he was talking about getting passengers out of the airplane or engines out of reverse. Anyway, we got the engines out of reverse and I quickly made an announcement for the passengers to stay seated, which also let the flight attendants know not to open the emergency exits and evacuate the airplane. I could just imagine three hundred people evacuating the aircraft onto the snowy airfield and our incident being reported on the evening news that day. Our next task was to figure out if we were still on the runway, which we soon confirmed that we were.

Working the complex DC-10 flight engineer panel

Captain J. B. managed to compose himself enough to taxi the aircraft to the assigned gate at Denver Stapleton Airport. Once parked at the gate and with passengers deplaned, Captain J. B. left the cockpit to make some phone calls and maybe to clean out his britches. After he returned to let us know everything was all right, he never showed any appreciation whatsoever. He didn't say "thanks," "good job," "well done," or anything like that. Overall, due to my quick thinking and First Officer Morse's courage to quickly do what was needed, we had saved the day and kept from having to evacuate the airplane and dump three hundred people in the snow. Also, we'd kept ole Captain J. B. from having a major FAA violation on his record.

I simply summed it all up as a lesson learned about how to be thankful and the wisdom not to expect thanks from anyone. How's that for a balanced approach to life circumstances? What's more is that I would be a flight engineer on two other flights with Captain J. B. when something went wrong. Once, the DC-10 we were parking at the Newark airport hit a tug. On another occasion, Captain J. B. nearly burned up an engine trying to get it started on a cold morning in Colorado Springs. Needless to say, I was glad when I eventually moved on from my troublesome DC-10 days. On the bright side, the absolute greatest highlight of my time on the mighty DC-10 was around 1990 when Mr. Clyde McGrady, my favorite high school teacher from Americus, was a passenger on one of my flights from Los Angeles to Chicago. He was oh so proud of me, his former student, that day and I was so very thankful for him having been a stern disciplinarian and a magnificent educator who cared dearly for his students.

By the way, during this time my Air Force Reserve unit was tasked with getting volunteers to deploy to the Middle East for Desert Shield. Saddam Hussein had invaded Kuwait and the United States was preparing for war with Iraq. Luckily for me, the commander of my unit found enough volunteers to deploy to the Middle East and I was ultimately spared having to go to a war zone. Frankly, I've always wondered why people in that part of the world have suffered so much violence and bloodshed? Could it be mainly motivated by entrenched fanatical religious differences dating back centuries? Overall, will you join in and say a prayer with me that someday all the people of the world who breathe the same air will settle on one basic belief system under one God that loves us all?

The potential of being called to active duty as I was struggling to recover from the divorce put tremendous stress on me. My smoking Black & Mild cigars and drinking alcohol increased during this time, and before long, I found myself having career-threatening medical issues. One day while on a layover in San Mateo, California, I was leisurely walking down the street smoking a Black & Mild cigar when a knot appeared on the side of my head in the temple area. Recognizing that this could be a deadly warning sign, I put out that cigar and never smoked another since that day. God spoke to me that day and let me know that if I didn't stop smoking Black & Milds, I would be Black and Dead!

Not surprisingly, my 1992 military flight physical revealed that I had glaucoma, and later, my blood pressure became elevated. Thus, I was taken off flight status and had to find a nonflying military position elsewhere. That's when I became an Air Force Academy liaison officer, where I recruited academy applicants and guided them through the appointment process. My new position helped me get beyond the twenty-year threshold to have more than enough time to retire from the Air Force Reserves. Fortunately, my health issues did not keep me from flying with United.

As I began to recover financially, I bought a brand-new black 1992 Pontiac Grand Prix and my oldest son, Curtis, who had just graduated from high school, came to live with me at my apartment. The plan was for Curtis to live with me and attend Atlanta Metro College. It was also a time for us to get to know each other better, which was long overdue. Soon, we relocated from my Dekalb County apartment to a lovely little house I bought in East Point. I really loved that house because it was a cozy place to live and convenient to the Atlanta airport and my reserve unit at Dobbins AFB. Unfortunately, the houses in East Point were way too close to each other and I had several issues with a white neighbor who didn't like my music, or much anything else I did. He would often call the East Point Police to complain about my music or anything that bothered him.

Retiring from the Air Force Reserves was vital to the goals I had in mind in my later years. Nevertheless, I wanted to retire with a higher rank. I had the time in grade as captain to be promoted to major, but for some reason the promotion was held up. Using the expert writing skills I had learned in college, I started writing letters to whomever I thought would help. Before long, I had reached the right people and got promoted to major around 1993.

My service as a liaison officer didn't last very long, but I did finally get the chance to visit the beautiful Air Force Academy in Colorado Springs in 1994. This sprawling campus in Colorado Springs sits just west of town and has breathtaking views of the towering Rocky Mountains close by. As I was touring the vast campus, I wondered to myself what it would have been like to spend four years there. Air Force Academy graduates are affectionately known as "zoomies," and a degree from that institution would have been oh so precious. In the meantime, I got word that my Uncle Bo had died. He was the only connection to my father I ever knew. My siblings and I had lost touch with him, and regrettably we never thought to get more information about our father's side of the family from him. Fortunately, I was able to help give him a proper burial at a cemetery near some railroad tracks in Butler, Georgia.

Soon, I decided to upgrade to Boeing 757/767 copilot, also known as first officer, to be based out of Chicago (ORD). This was my very first time flying in a pilot seat at United Airlines. The 757 is what is called a narrow-body, single-aisle airliner, while the 767 is a wide-body, dual-aisle airliner. In my opinion, the 757 is perhaps the best airliner ever made. No other airliner has the capacity to carry the same load and operate into most airports like the 757 does. My initial operating experience (IOE) was with a superb instructor pilot named Al Calvalero. Al had just come off sick leave, but too soon to fully recover from the flu he had been suffering from. The first flight of my IOE was a night flight from

Chicago to Fort Lauderdale and Al wanted me to fly because he still had chills from the flu. But he put me in a peculiar position that night because we were assigned to fly a 767-300, which was bigger than any airplane I had ever flown.

At the major airlines, the first time a new pilot fresh out of training gets to fly in a real airplane is on a revenue flight with real passengers on board. I assessed the situation like this: I had never flown a 767 and had never flown into Fort Lauderdale, so I told Al he was going to have to fly that leg because I simply wasn't comfortable flying that huge airplane yet. Thankfully, he was able to get us to Fort Lauderdale that night and I became familiar enough with the airplane to fly it on another day. Fortunately for me, most of my trips were on the 757 flying coast-to-coast transcontinental flights. Around this time, I started seriously considering transferring to Washington, DC. (IAD) and moving to the area. I had made the sacrifice up to this point to stay near my sons and family and commute to Chicago. Meanwhile, I had been in and out of a few relationships, but there was one lady who caught my eye. At some point I had read in a book that I should create a list of qualities I want in a wife, pray about it, and patiently wait for her to show up.

Alice and I at a banquet

The first time I saw Alice was at a fashion show at the Atlanta Airport Renaissance Hotel. I had gone to the fashion show to support the effort to raise funds to save Morris Brown College, which was in serious financial trouble. I could see that this woman I called a "fine fox" was extremely busy managing the event, so I kept my distance and watched her from afar. Somehow, I knew there would be another opportunity to approach her.

That opportunity came at the Omega fraternity house in southwest Atlanta, a popular nightspot. She was extremely good-looking, and a great dancer, so I asked her to dance on several occasions as she passed me by on her way back to her table. Each time she would look me squarely in the face and say, *"No!"* Usually, I wouldn't ever approach a woman a second time if she rejected me like that, but something made me try again and again.

After reading more about how to approach a woman you're interested in, I decided to try a different approach. I had learned the best way to gain someone's attention was to find something you have in common and use that as a means of introduction. One night, I spotted Alice sitting alone at that same popular night spot called the Omega Frat House and made my move. I approached and asked, "Didn't I see you at a fashion show a year or so ago?"

To my surprise she said, "Yes," and I was able to begin a cordial conversation that led to a lasting relationship.

I learned that Alice had a master's of business administration degree (MBA), which she had proudly earned while living in Florida. She was employed by the State of Florida as a tax auditor and traveled to do audits at companies around the southeast. Alice had moved to Georgia from the Tampa/St. Petersburg area somewhere around 1990 and had recently bought a house in Riverdale. In addition to her unique beauty, what really stood out about her was her amazing level of charm in addition to her awareness and intelligence. Most notably, she was someone who pushed me to get physically fit and learn much more about religion. Overall, it has been very rewarding to have met and married a woman who motivates me, challenges me, and helps me stay healthy.

During our year of courtship, Alice only got the chance to see my mother in the hospital, as she was getting very ill. That last time we visited her in the hospital, my mother seemed to give her nod of approval, and our relationship got serious. On a visit to Americus to show her where I grew up, I took her to see where my father is buried, where for some strange reason the alarm on her car mysteriously went off. Perhaps that was my dad's approval too.

We spent a great deal of time together and both enjoyed shopping and listening to smooth jazz music as well. Realizing we had both been in failed marriages before, premarital counseling was a must if we were to have any chance at a successful marriage. Alice was a member of New Birth Missionary Baptist and I had joined the church too. We attended marriage counseling for several weeks, which gave us a good foundation for our marital relationship. On March 18, 1995, we got married, which happened to be the same day I had graduated from pilot training in 1982. Interestingly, Bishop Eddie Long performed our marriage ceremony.

For decades, I had been deeply troubled by lingering episodes of racism and how little I knew about Black history. I began searching for books about Black History to educate myself on the intimate details of how my ancestors had come to America from Africa to be sold into slavery. On every airline trip, I tried to find a bookstore where I could find any book of interest. One book, entitled *The Historical and Cultural Atlas of African Americans* by Molefi Ashante and Mark T. Mattson, really opened my eyes to how the cruel enslavement and prolonged oppression of my ancestors caused extensive multigenerational psychological damage that continues today. I concluded that descendants of enslaved Americans desperately needed a unique identity and flag to instill pride among our people. The vivid memories of reciting the Pledge of Allegiance in elementary school while my people were in the streets protesting segregation remained ever present all those years. So, I proudly created the name AFRICAMERICA and a flag to go with it. AFRICAMERICA is simply a merging of the words Africa and America, which is symbolic of our African heritage and our American legacy of struggling for freedom, equality, and justice. My ultimate goal was to someday build an AFRICAMERICA resort or park where African Americans could go to relax in an Afrocentric cultural atmosphere with soul and smooth jazz music being played throughout the venue.

The Jet Will Fly!

The AFRICAMERICA flag

Flying back and forth to another city to start my airline trips was no fun, and I lost a lot of time doing this. Before getting married, I had seriously considered moving to Washington, DC, to avoid commuting back and forth. The deciding factor was my mother's failing health, and eventually she passed away in April 1995. Just by coincidence, I was alone with her in the hospital room as she lay in a semiconscious state, moaning in pain. Knowing she was in so much pain, all I could do was say, "Jesus, help my mother," over and over again until I heard her clench her teeth and let out a long sigh. Just like that, the woman who brought me into this world was gone—forever. The only parent I had ever really known had left us, and the stark reality of being without any parent was sobering. Fortunately, having Alice in my life was comforting, and we made the decision to continue living in the Atlanta area.

Thereafter in 1995, I recognized that I had had enough of military service, counted my blessings, and submitted the necessary paperwork to retire. By the grace of God, I had had a very rewarding military career that began as the tumultuous Vietnam War was winding down and ended as the Gulf War conflicts in the Middle East were heating up. Now, all I had to do was live beyond age sixty to reap the full benefits of being a retired reservist. Around that time, my son Curtis developed a desire to continue his education elsewhere, so he decided to transfer to Fort Valley State College in Ft. Valley, Georgia. This move allowed him to mature, become more responsible, and meet his lovely wife, Tramicha.

I turned my attention to moving on to larger aircraft, as United Airlines was taking delivery of brand-new Boeing 777s. I made the decision to keep my residence in the Atlanta area and to transfer so I could fly out of Washington, DC, to be a first officer on that aircraft. About the same time, I sold my cherished East Point home and moved into my wife's house in Riverdale, Georgia. Thereafter, we made plans to buy a nice lot and some house plans to build our dream home in Fayette County Georgia.

Building a house is a monumental project, especially for a newlywed couple. There are hundreds of decisions that need to be made, and the builder has to be monitored to make sure things turn out right. Our marriage was put to the test as we dealt with the numerous decisions we needed to make. Thankfully, we managed to find the ability to compromise and get it done. It definitely wasn't easy. We did a lot of praying, too, which is essential to making marriage work under any circumstance. As with flying, prayer and compromise are essential to a balanced life as a whole.

Being on the 777 allowed me to be home a lot because the airplane was new. That meant there were times my trips would be taken for training, and I got to stay home and still get paid. This was one of the best parts of being an airline pilot. The other best

The Jet Will Fly!

part was something called vacation override. If any part of your vacation touched a trip you were assigned, the whole trip would be dropped, and you got paid. Several times, I got the entire month off using vacation override. Most of my trips on the 777 were between Washington Dulles and European cities like London, Paris, Frankfurt, Amsterdam, and Brussels.

Some of the early London trips had fifty-two-hour layovers as opposed to the usual twenty-four hours. On one particular fifty-two-hour layover in London, I got what I think was food poisoning after dining out with my crew members at a local restaurant. I came down with a protracted condition that had me alternating between chills, fever, and vomiting. I spent the remainder of my layover in my room. When I informed my captain before the return flight to Dulles Airport, he said I should have informed someone on the crew that I was sick. He was absolutely right, because I could have died, and no one would have known until it was time for us to fly back home.

I never really got too comfortable flying twin-engine airplanes over the vast Atlantic Ocean. When crossing the Atlantic Ocean, we always had to have a diversion or emergency airport in mind to divert to just in case an engine failed or had to be shut down. That's why in 1998 I decided to become a 747-400 first officer. For the most part, I loved flying the 747-400, a huge four-engine jumbo jet that had a maximum takeoff weight of 875,000 pounds and a range of about sixteen to eighteen hours of flight time. My very first 747 landing was in Osaka, Japan, at an airport that had actually been constructed and built in the ocean next to the city. Thereafter, I had initial operating experience (IOE) flights to Tokyo, Japan, and Seoul, South Korea.

After IOE, I was initially based out of New York (JFK) and flew primarily to Tokyo. On these ultra long range twelve to sixteen or more hour flights, the four-pilot crew featured a captain, first officer, and two inflight relief pilots to allow for required rest breaks in the bunk beds on board. After flying as the first officer on a few flights, I opted to mainly fly as an inflight relief pilot because the six-day trip was way too long to be away from home. The trips included a thirteen-hour flight from New York to Tokyo with a crew of four and a twenty-four-hour layover there. The next day the captain and first officer flew a seven-hour Tokyo-to-Singapore flight. In my opinion, that flight was extremely exhausting and downright dangerous because your sleep cycle was so out of whack. I recall that by the time we neared Singapore, my captain and I could barely stay awake to get that jumbo jet safely on the ground.

Luckily, I quickly transferred to Chicago (ORD), where I flew mostly as a relief pilot on sixteen-hour flights to Hong Kong. Some of those flights were over the North Pole, which typically shaved about forty-five minutes off the flight. The first time I ever laid over in Hong Kong, I was amazed at this unique former British colony and English-speaking city. It  was fascinating and unlike any city in the world I had ever seen. Hong Kong is a sprawling city that spans from a hilly peninsula to an island separated by a super busy harbor, and the city has what seems like thousands of huge skyscrapers. We stayed in a first-class hotel that sits right next to the busy Victoria Harbour. I thoroughly enjoyed the shopping, walking all over the city, and taking the ferry across to the harbor.

Because of the length of my flights, I usually had anywhere from eighteen to twenty-one days off a month. This allowed me time to work on my AFRICAMERICA ideas and to get involved with the local NAACP in Fayette County that I helped start. With a Black population of around thirteen percent, Fayette County was in dire need of a strong NAACP branch to counteract the entrenched racial bias that pervaded every aspect of our lives. Thanks to the Rev. Nelson Rivers III, who was the field director for the NAACP southeast region, we were able to start building a local organization that would become a force for equality and inclusion. One of my early roles was working in membership, publicity, and political action. Becoming active with the NAACP provided me the necessary work/life balance I needed. Furthermore, being active with the NAACP came from the repressed desire to continue my interest in civil rights that had stemmed from that childhood march I participated in long ago.

The captain who trained me to fly the 747 warned me not to stay on it too long, because most pilots like me, who flew mostly as relief pilots, hardly ever got more than three to six landings a year in the actual airplane. At my wife's urging, I decided to take my first captain bid on the 757/767 in 2000 after the union representing our pilots negotiated the largest pay raise we had ever had. This meant giving up my seniority as a copilot and being at a position of lower seniority in the left seat. This also meant being on call once again since my early days at the airline. In November 2000, I trained to become a 757/767 captain at the Denver Flight training center.

The 757 was to me the most beautiful airliner ever built, and I had always wanted to be a captain on it. Most of the 757 aircraft I flew had 24 first-class seats and 158 coach seats. The 757 could fly coast to coast with a full load of passengers, bags, and cargo, and we routinely could climb to forty thousand feet to get over much of the thunderstorms that were often in our path. When it came to stopping, the 757 had excellent braking with eight sets of brakes working for you versus four, like on a 737 or Airbus A320/319. Simply put, it was an awesome passenger jet to fly, and it could even land itself in zero visibility using the triple-channel CAT III ILS autoland system. Unlike any other airline fleet, a 757 pilot was often dual qualified on the wide body 767 as well. The two aircraft had their own unique flying and landing characteristics, and you always had to remember how to land each one. Not only did the two airliners have differences, but amazingly, 757/767 pilots had the best range of flying, with domestic and international routes to some great destinations.

Recognizing that I was entering the most stressful part of my career as an airline pilot, I began to go to the gym and jog on the treadmill whenever I could. It was my understanding that physical exercise was essential to alleviating the stress and strain of being an airline captain. I would routinely run on the treadmill for an hour or more in order to stay physically fit. The regular exercise and the discipline to study hard made the six weeks of training bearable. Thankfully, sitting in the copilot seat for six years had prepared me well to be a captain. The bad captains had given me the motivation not to be like them, and I eagerly adopted the traits of the good captains I had flown with.

Every now and then someone would ask me how I felt about being responsible for all those lives. I would tell them that as long as I got myself to the appointed destination safely, everybody else would be all right, so I never worried about things going wrong.

As a captain, you are, of course, expected to know how to safely operate the aircraft, manage the crew, and effectively handle every problem that crops up. You are also expected to know the intimate details about everything from how the systems on the airplane work to the multitude of FAA regulations that govern flying to numerous company rules to various other policies and procedures wherever in the world you are scheduled to fly.

Overall, being an airline pilot, and particularly an airline captain, means realizing that you can never know everything you are supposed to know, but you are responsible for knowing it anyway. It was a heavy burden to bear, but here's the most important lesson I learned: The biggest lesson about becoming a captain and wearing four stripes on your shoulders was to be a strong leader with the knowledge and ability to focus on the big stuff that matters most. Everything else will take care of itself. That's how I overcame the weight of becoming a captain with the goal of serving my passengers and crew to the best of my abilities.

Captain's Authority

BEING A CAPTAIN is the highlight of an airline pilot's career. It's a time when a pilot is trusted with the safe and efficient operation of an aircraft during all sorts of demanding, and sometimes dangerous, conditions. As a captain for United Airlines, I took this obligation very seriously, and that's why my career was so successful.

My early months as captain on the 757/767 were spent mostly sitting on reserve in hotels in the Washington Dulles area. I was delighted to fly transcontinental flights because I was able to read numerous books while crisscrossing the United States, mostly on four-day trips to the West Coast and primarily to California. On one particular West Coast trip, we had a layover in Santa Ana, California (SNA). Santa Ana was a dangerous airport to operate a 757 in and out of due to the shortness of the runway and noise abatement restrictions that called for an unusually steep climb to 1,500 feet on takeoff toward the Pacific Ocean. When landing at SNA, you had to be extremely diligent about looking for and avoiding small Cessna-type aircraft that flew in and around the airport area too. When landing there, a pilot had to have the aircraft on the ground in the first 500 feet and use maximum brakes and reverse thrust in order to stop before the runway ran out.

One day, I had a new female first officer, and we were scheduled to fly from Santa Ana to San Francisco early one morning. I was flying and we had an airplane with a deferred maintenance item on the equipment cooling system. After reviewing the maintenance deferral, something didn't seem quite right, but I accepted the aircraft after being assured by the maintenance personnel. With me at the controls, I started the takeoff roll, and as soon as we took off and started climbing, we got a caution message on the center instrument panel: EQUIPMENT COOLING. I immediately instructed my copilot to refer to the flight manual to see what the procedure was to take care of the problem. As she worked through the steps in the manual, I continued to fly the aircraft and let air traffic control know we were working on a problem. As we climbed higher through about twenty thousand feet, I noticed the instruments in front of me started to dim and I knew things were getting worse.

Instinctively, I transferred control to my copilot and took the manual to see if she had finished it completely. To my surprise, the last step read, *LAND AT THE NEAREST SUITABLE AIRPORT!* A radio conversation with our centralized maintenance department on the ground also convinced me that we had a serious problem on our hands. That was when I told the air traffic controller we were declaring an inflight emergency. The controller asked the usual questions such as, "Say number of souls on board and fuel remaining." Years later, it occurred to me that air traffic controllers need to know how many "souls" are on board because no matter what happens, souls are never lost.

Next, the controller wanted to know our intentions and, at first, I started to tell them we planned to divert to Los Angeles, which we had just flown over, headed north to our destination. On the other hand, we were at twenty-five thousand feet traveling at about five hundred knots and about two hundred miles from San Francisco. I figured that since we would be able to get to San Francisco about the same time we could spiral down and land at Los Angeles, it was best to continue on. So, I made my first major decision in a midair crisis situation and landed at the San Francisco airport without incident.

The most interesting thing that occurred was the maintenance people discovered that the contract mechanic at SNA had failed to properly configure the equipment cooling system. So instead of fixing the system, they told me a United mechanic at San Francisco Airport had reconfigured the aircraft to fly with an alternate procedure and tried to get me to fly the same airplane to our next destination. I boldly refused. I said, "Y'all got to fix that airplane before I fly it again!" So, they had no choice but to fix it or give us another airplane because, thanks to my union, the Air Line Pilots Association (ALPA), the airline could not force a pilot to fly an airplane the pilot deemed unsafe to fly. We were assigned another 757 and flew on to our destination that day. Early in my career as a captain, I had learned yet another lesson in how to overcome the weight of the world: Never fly an airplane that has an unresolved issue or condition you are not comfortable with.

During my first few years as a 757/767 captain, a lot of things happened on and off the job. On the job, I flew to places like São Paulo, Brazil; Honolulu, Hawaii; and numerous places in Europe. My goal was to try to fly domestic trips every chance I got because I never really liked flying to international destinations. I never liked changing money into other currencies, eating foreign food, watching foreign television, or trying to communicate in other languages. That was why I didn't mind flying to London, England, because at least I could speak the language. I'm glad I was able to be assigned to fly mostly domestic trips.

Up until 1994, I had never been at the controls of a large commercial airliner. I had spent over five years as a flight engineer sitting at a panel behind the two pilots. Flying complex jet airplanes is a rare privilege and a tremendous challenge, especially when you are the captain. Perhaps that's why few people have the desire or aptitude to learn to fly commercial airliners for a living. Furthermore, learning to fly is extremely expensive, unless you're fortunate enough to be trained by the military. Taking off is fairly easy especially if the wind is calm, but on the other hand, landings are always challenging, especially when the wind is gusty. Thus, it is extremely satisfying when a pilot can make a smooth landing in demanding conditions like landing in a thirty-knot crosswind. I recall numerous times landing at some of the most difficult or busiest airports in the country. LaGuardia in New York, Washington National in DC, Santa Ana in Orange County, San Francisco Airport in California, Denver Airport in Colorado, and O'Hare Airport in Illinois are just a few airfields that require the utmost expertise from a pilot.

My first landing at LaGuardia was with an FAA examiner on board in the jump seat, and I was assigned to fly the Expressway Visual Approach to runway 31. This is one of the most dreaded approaches because it requires a pilot to visually acquire and follow the Long Island Expressway to the east while flying at about three thousand feet. Pilots have to configure with flaps out and landing gear down to slow the aircraft for landing while looking for a racetrack to turn toward the airport. As the aircraft makes a descending turn at low airspeed, you come close to some apartment buildings as you roll out on final aiming for the touchdown zone. As soon as you touch down, the automatic brakes kick in and you use full reverse thrust to come to a stop before the intersecting runway.

On busy days, as soon as your aircraft was assured to not cross the intersecting runway, the air traffic controller would clear a departing aircraft to take off on runway 4. On another occasion, I remember landing there on runway 22 one rainy and stormy night with a strong, gusty crosswind. That 757 was rocking and rolling down the final approach as I jockeyed the throttles to maintain approach airspeed, which was higher than usual because of the gusty winds. As my heartbeat increased with the energy it took to stay on course and on speed, we broke out of the clouds and I focused on the touchdown zone. On every approach, and especially on approaches like this, pilots are always primed to be ready to go around and try another approach. Even so, I was keenly focused on landing in those rocky and turbulent conditions that night.

At about two hundred feet before touchdown, a gust of wind from the right began to push the aircraft off course. I instinctively added power, lowered the right wing with the left rudder, and flared the aircraft, making a smooth touchdown and then immediately applying maximum reverse thrust on the engines. As I reflect on that nearly impossible approach and landing, I must admit that at one point it seemed like me and Jesus were flying that 757, because everything rapidly came together to arrive at a successful outcome that night and on a few other occasions too.

Throughout my flying career with United, there were other various incidents that helped me realize God was always watching over me. There was the occasional near midair collision with small airplanes that were not under the guidance of air traffic control. Pilots must always be safety-conscious and constantly search for other airplanes that pose a collision threat, especially when descending or climbing out of airports. There were encounters with severe thunderstorms that we had to always be prepared to navigate around using our radar and good instincts.

An aircraft I was flying into Boston one stormy night was struck by lightning, which was dissipated out to the wing and tail by design. All we experienced was some momentary interference with our flight instruments. There was another stormy night in Chicago when multiple lines of vicious thunderstorm had shut down departures. Several other aircraft were sitting on the ramp along with us and we all had our engines shut down to conserve fuel. In between two waves of storms, an air traffic controller asked if anyone wanted to try departing to the west. My copilot and I carefully assessed the weather conditions to the west, as we had been sitting on the ramp for hours waiting to take off for California.

We could see the constant lightning and plotted a course that seemed to take us around and in between the bad weather. We agreed to try it, started our engines, and rolled out to the runway to make another assessment of the weather. Feeling comfortable with the path we planned, we took off into the dark and stormy night heading west. It was extremely turbulent as we rocked and rolled on our way up to thirty-five thousand feet. I clearly recall watching multiple lightning bolts flash on either side of the aircraft as we skillfully navigated through a maze of towering thunderstorm cells. Was it scary? Of course it was scary! Nevertheless, I had little time to be scared because people were depending on me to get them to their intended destination. By the grace of God, that was what I did time and time again.

All pilots are trained to avoid flying through convective thunderstorms, and for good reason. Few pilots have flown through towering thunderstorms and lived to talk about it. Golf ball- or softball-sized hail produced by thunderstorms have destroyed jet engines and caused airplanes to crash-land with tragic consequences. Other unfortunate pilot encounters with thunderstorms have ripped the wings off airplanes and caused them to crash, killing everyone on board. Needless to say, I had developed a healthy respect for thunderstorms and convective weather. Another flying hazard for airliners was mountain waves. Strong air currents associated with the jet stream at high altitudes can cause an airliner to become unstable and drop hundreds of feet in an instant.

We always had to watch out for significant airspeed and altitude fluctuations especially associated with turbulence. Light to moderate turbulence was another frequent hazard. Rarely have I ever flown a coast-to-coast flight without encountering some level of turbulence. Once, I encountered what appeared to be unexpected severe turbulence descending into Denver International Airport. Fortunately, I had turned on the seatbelt sign and told the flight attendants to take their seats early before we got rocked pretty good. Passengers have been killed when airliners flew through severe turbulence without warning. The Denver Airport is infamous for strong winds that create something called windshear, or microburst.

I remember landing at the Denver Airport on runway 16L in gusty winds and with a windshear alert. At about three hundred feet, that 757 lost airspeed and started falling out of the sky fast. I pushed the throttles up toward maximum power for about half a second and then rapidly pulled them back to idle just as fast. The momentary thrust on the engines generated just enough power to arrest the sink rate just in time for me to flare the aircraft and touch down ever so gently, as I had done so many other times. Most of all, my goal was to never get anybody hurt by turbulence, or in any other way for that matter.

In the wintertime, airframe and engine icing were other frequent threats we had to counter in addition to deicing the aircraft in snowy conditions on the ground before takeoff. And on those trips down to South America during the wee hours of the night, we would have to watch closely for hard-to-spot dry-top thunderstorms that were always lingering around the equator near Colombia.

There were other serious issues I had to deal with as a captain. Before Captain Sully had his run-in with a flock of birds at LaGuardia Airport in New York, I had a similar incident happen while departing the Houston Airport. On takeoff roll with the co-pilot at the controls, I was routinely monitoring the engines for any sign of trouble before our V1 (go or no-go speed) when the copilot yelled, "Birds!" I glanced up to see a large flock of seagulls flying directly in front of us. To our amazement, every single bird missed hitting that 757 as we climbed through the flock. No one can tell me God wasn't watching over us and everyone on board. If those birds had hit the aircraft and taken out our engines, we wouldn't have had the option to land in a river like Sully did. We probably would have crashed straight ahead into trees or the buildings off the end of the runway, and you wouldn't be reading this book right now.

As a pilot, I also had to deal with airline management that tries to find ways to cut cost, usually at the expense of safety. One such example was an effort to get pilots to fly with less fuel to save the airline money. This was during a time when fuel costs were very high and airline profits were suffering. I even had to attend a mandatory fuel-management class where I was essentially urged not to add fuel above what the dispatcher determined to be sufficient for the flight. To me, this was downright stupid, dangerous, and extremely stressful to pilots. It became real to me when I had to fly a red-eye from Los Angeles to Washington Dulles one night.

Naturally I was defiant, and actually added additional fuel even though the arrival weather was forecast to be clear. I just never felt comfortable flying with only enough fuel to get to my destination, plus the usual forty-five-minute additional fuel for reserves or unexpected (short) delays. As we approached our descent for landing at Washington that next morning, the air traffic controller put us in a holding pattern for unexplained reasons. We told the controller we couldn't hold for long and started looking at diverting to Richmond, Virginia, or Pittsburg, Pennsylvania. After a few turns in the holding pattern, the controller cleared us to fly toward Washington, but later put us in another unexpected holding pattern near the airport. By now, we didn't have enough fuel to divert anywhere, so we were about to declare emergency fuel, which would compel the controller to let us fly directly to the destination airport and land.

On final approach, our fuel got so low that the LOW FUEL warning message appeared on the panel in front of us. This required turning on all fuel pumps and planning to land without having to go around. Fortunately, we made an uneventful landing at Washington Dulles Airport and parked at the gate with very little fuel left in our tanks. That was when I said that would never happen again. From then on, I would always have enough fuel on board to make myself as comfortable as the CEO sitting in his cushy desk chair at corporate headquarters. The job of an airline pilot is stressful enough without having to try to save a few pennies by flying with less fuel. Ironically, there was one white captain who was notorious for trying to fly with less fuel. In conversations with the copilots who flew with him, I was told they had to tell him they wouldn't get on the airplane if he took fuel off or declined to add fuel when it might be needed.

Sadly, I did have to deal with flying with white co-pilots who obviously didn't care to fly with a Black captain. They would do annoying things like make various requests over the radio without coordinating with me. Or they would work on crossword puzzles or read a newspaper without paying attention to the aircraft. Sometimes they would miss radio calls or forget to switch frequencies, which was not a good thing to do. The most disturbing event was when a white copilot turned off the engine anti-ice without asking me as we were descending through clouds into the Denver Airport. This was in addition to several other things he had done to annoy me. When we landed, I had had enough.

After the aircraft was parked at the gate and the passengers had deplaned, I turned to the copilot and told him I was going to make a call to crew scheduling to request a new copilot. You should have seen the look on his face. At first, he got defensive, but then realized he had a choice to make. He had to either agree to stop being insubordinate or go home. After that talk, he decided he would respect the captain's authority like he was supposed to. When operating complex airliners, pilots must have a clear understanding of how to work together. Prior to my becoming an airline pilot, there had been several crashes because pilots were uncooperative or disrespectful toward each other.

The airlines eventually embraced something called Human Factors, which examines the root causes of airline crashes. And because of the great work done by scientists studying behavioral problems, airline operators also started using something called Crew Resource Management (CRM). This is why you rarely hear about airliners crashing these days. This goes on to show that with the right amount of motivation and focus, humankind can be trained to stop doing things that get people hurt or killed. Most of all, it also means ordinary people can be trained not to harm or shoot others if there is enough interest in modifying those behaviors. Wouldn't that be great?

Off the job, George W. Bush had managed to become president of the United States of America. I thought he was the worst president ever. The Republican Party had used every trick in the book to cheat and steal the presidency. After becoming president, the Bush administration proceeded to dismantle the programs that benefited Black people that President Bill Clinton had put in place. I dreaded the fact that a Republican was president, because I had suffered under every Republican president since Nixon. On September 10, 2001, I had returned from a trip to Milan, Italy, and had flown home from Washington Dulles to Atlanta on the jump seat of a Delta flight. I awakened at home the next day and turned on the television that morning, September 11, 2001. I gazed in disbelief at the video replay of the first aircraft crashing into the World Trade Center tower at 8:46 a.m. and heard the reporter say they thought a small plane had accidentally crashed into the building.

The Jet Will Fly!

SEPTEMBER MOURNING

The year was two thousand one, September eleven the day
The devil took flight that morning and came flying our way

Such a beautiful day it was with its skies clear and bright
Off to work so many went never to come home that night

Like bats out of hell jetliners barreled out of the blue sky
Smashing into things causing many innocent people to die

In the end great buildings burned, buckled, and some fell
Evil had got up that morning and escaped the gates of hell

Days would pass before anyone knew the final human toll
America began to fight back when a hero said, "Let's Roll"

Terrorism came home that day and instilled fear and fright
Like a hateful lynch mob or klan in the middle of the night

Search your soul to see the message this day has for us all
United we shall overcome and divided we stumble and fall

May we never forget what happened to our country that day
Always remember to get down on your knees, bow and pray

God bless America with liberty, equality and justice for all
Correct its faults, protect it from harm and never let it fall.

John E. Jones
11 September 2002

© John E. Jones 2002

I thought to myself, *It's highly unlikely that an airplane would accidentally crash into a building in New York City. This can't be an accident.* Soon thereafter, the second airplane, a United Airlines 767, came barreling out of the sky aiming at the second Twin Tower. At 9:02 a.m., that second huge airliner smashed into the tower right before my eyes. I sat there in my bedroom watching these horrific events take place and wondered what the future held. Soon it was announced that two other airliners had been hijacked too. One reportedly crashed into the Pentagon, and the attempt to hijack the other airliner was thwarted when it crashed into a field in Pennsylvania. The Twin Towers burned for hours, and one by one pancaked to the ground.

I was so saddened at the multitude of people who lost their lives that day and wondered how many would die or be maimed for life. All non-military aircraft airborne that day were ordered to land at the nearest airport, and many airliners were stuck wherever they landed that day. It was then I realized how fortunate I was to have been at home. But how would this tragic chain of events affect my career as an airline pilot? Many junior pilots were put on furlough, where they would remain for years. I soon realized that as a junior 757/767 captain I wouldn't be furloughed, but I would be stuck on reserve or on call for a very long time. Since I was a commuter pilot, that would mean having to stay in hotels more often because all the airlines cut back on flights dramatically. The future of all the airlines also became uncertain because they had excessive cash burn and less revenue. It was a matter of time before United Airlines would file for bankruptcy and possibly go out of business.

As for me, staying in hotels around Dulles Airport became very expensive. It was time to seriously evaluate my options. Moving to the Washington Dulles Airport area while not knowing if my airline would survive was risky. So, I decided to search for a home away from home. My real estate agent found this charming two-bedroom one-and-a-half-bath condo within fifteen minutes driving time to Dulles. After conferring with my wife Alice, I decided to buy the condo so I would have my own home away from home and not have to waste money in hotels. This condo also became an appreciating investment and allowed me to explore the Washington DC area as well. Meanwhile, the war on terrorism expanded beyond fighting the Taliban in Afghanistan. Bush and the Republicans seemed to be so desperate to coerce Congress and the American public into invading Iraq that they manufactured evidence to make it happen. This is further proof that today's Republican Party is woefully corrupt. My distaste for the Bush administration became almost unbearable as it started looking more and more like they had created the conditions that led to 9/11. How else would Congress have approved of funding the so-called war on terrorism?

Before long, United Airlines declared bankruptcy and we pilots took drastic pay cuts to save the airline. In the process, we also lost our Employee Stock Ownership Plan (ESOP), which could have made me a multimillionaire by the time I retired. Our main pension plan was terminated and turned over to the government program called the Pension Benefit Guarantee Corporation (PBGC). That meant we pilots would get about two-thirds of what we would have gotten at the current mandatory retirement at sixty years of age. United Airlines CEO Glenn Tilton, who was brought in to manage the airline through the crisis, apparently got a bonus for getting us pilots to take those drastic pay cuts. I was absolutely furious. I then realized CEOs can be some of the most greedy, ruthless, and heartless people to ever walk the face of the earth. Maybe that's why I developed an interest in airline management. Perhaps I could move up through the ranks and treat employees better. I applied for my first management position as a flight manager around 2004 and was interviewed by my supervisor, who was my chief pilot. Needless to say, I was turned down, but a few other Black pilots did get to move up to low-level management positions. Because of this, I felt somewhat hopeful.

Back at home in Fayette County, I remained active with my local NAACP branch. I also decided to make a run for an open seat as a Georgia state representative for my local area and delved into other interests I had. My efforts with the NAACP focused on getting the word out about the branch and building membership. All the while, I was learning more and more about Black history and the effectiveness of the NAACP in bringing about change for African Americans. I soon became interested in figuring out how to bring district voting to Fayette County so a Black candidate would have a fairer chance to get elected in a county where all county commissioners and school board members were elected by voters from all over the county. This made it virtually impossible for a person of color to get elected, yet the white establishment couldn't care less.

In 2006, I led local efforts to support the extension of the Voting Rights Act, which was eventually given a twenty-five-year extension. Unbeknownst to many, the Voting Rights Act has been responsible for helping thousands of Black candidates get elected because it provides a fairer way to elect government leaders. It was then I realized I would have to become branch president to help spearhead the effort to bring district voting to Fayette County Georgia.

In 2004, I had stepped away from NAACP activities to run for state representative. I ran against three other candidates, one of whom was an ambitious and well-connected Black woman. She ultimately won the seat and I graciously returned to my civic activities in my community and with the NAACP. A lot of lessons were learned, and it seems running for political office is for those who are willing to do absolutely anything to win or stay in office. I just wanted to serve my community at the state level, but not enough people in my district voted for me. Furthermore, losing a political race is a serious blow to the ego, and it took some time to recover from that.

In 2008, I became Fayette County branch president when the former president resigned in the midst of a contentious time for our branch. Somehow, I knew this would happen; I just didn't know how or when. Despite fending off some major challenges by some very egotistical people who wanted to take the branch in a different direction, I won reelection and went on to serve until 2016. Thanks to a book entitled *Power vs. Force* by David R. Hawkins, and other self-help books, I was able to use some amazing psychological techniques to overcome the weight of the world as some of my own Black people tried to interfere with my efforts to carry out my duties as president.

There's so much power in being nonreactive to people who

attack you or try to bring you down. I actually learned to love my enemies as Dr. Martin Luther King Jr. had learned to do, and the rewards are immeasurable. This also helped when I began to strongly advocate for the United States government to issue an official apology to African Americans. I cannot say for sure if my efforts made a difference, but soon after I sent letters to Senate Leader Harry Reid and House Majority Leader Nancy Pelosi, separate resolutions apologizing to African Americans were passed in each body of government. Unfortunately, the two houses of government were unable to reconcile the different versions, and that's where it stands to this day. Furthermore, the so-called apology never got any meaningful publicity and has no real ability to remedy the damage done by more than two hundred forty years of slavery, one hundred years of segregation, and another sixty years of struggle for real equality and justice.

The year 2009 brought about some promising developments that gave me tremendous hope. Barack Obama became the first Black president of the United States of America, and at first, I was so thankful. On the other hand, I wasn't as hopeful or excited as I should have been, for some strange reason. Somehow, I knew deep down his presidency probably wouldn't be as promising as it seemed. My instincts would prove me right years later. The inability of the Obama administration to oversee the dire need to advocate for fixing the Voting Rights Act was a colossal mistake and a major oversight that haunts us to this day. The failure to enact laws that would prohibit voter suppression directly led to Donald Trump becoming the forty-fifth president of the United States. Nevertheless, I wholeheartedly believe everything that happens has to happen.

The most delightful thing that came about in Obama's early years in office was United Airlines' decision to start flying 767s from Washington Dulles, where I was based, to Accra, Ghana. Because President Obama had visited Ghana during his first year in office, United Airlines management must have been convinced to start serving the African continent. The five-day trip to Ghana would be combined with a turnaround flight on the second day of the trip to Lagos, Nigeria, to load up on cheap fuel and return to Accra that night. The layover in Accra was at the plush resort known as Labadi Beach.

Crewmembers working flights to Ghana had to prepare by taking a series of shots and malaria pills. Captains who had never flown the route had to fly over with an instructor pilot who had to make sure special procedures were followed. Fortunately for me, I had an excellent instructor by the name of Captain Tony Green on that flight, and he, too, was Black like me. Flights from Washington Dulles to Accra took off around eleven in the evening and headed out on the eleven-hour flight over the Atlantic Ocean, coasting out usually somewhere around Wilmington, North Carolina. Flying through pitch darkness at thirty-five thousand feet, pilots had to be extra careful to avoid embedded thunderstorms, much like we had to do flying to South America.

As I took my first flight across the middle of the Atlantic Ocean, I couldn't help thinking about all the lost souls who didn't make it during the many crossings that brought millions of enslaved Africans through the Middle Passage to America between the 1600s and 1800s. When I arrived on African soil for the first time, it was if I had come home to the place where my ancestors had come from. It's a feeling that cannot be adequately put in words.

I would get to fly there a total of nine times between 2009 and 2012. During layovers, I got to tour the city of Accra, shop, and most importantly travel two hours west to Cape Coast to visit the place where captured Africans were rounded up and prepared for export to America. I also visited the center named for Dr. W. E. B. Du Bois in Accra. It was touching to see where he is buried and the rug at his gravesite that bears the logo of Clark Atlanta University, the school I graduated from.

Overall, the food in Africa was great, but crewmembers were warned never to drink water from the tap. Unlike the native Africans, our Americanized bodies and systems are not accustomed to the harmful microorganisms in the water there, so we were provided bottled water instead. As fate would have it, I must have used some tap water to rinse my toothbrush, and I got hold of a virus or something that made me very sick. I was vomiting and suffering from chills so bad that death was starting to look like a favorable option. Luckily for me, I was thoughtful enough to bring some vitamin packets with electrolytes in them that you mix with water. I put some in my water bottle and kept hydrating myself with it, and by the next day I was beginning to recover. By the grace of God, the flight I was scheduled to fly the next day to Lagos was cancelled, because it took me a while to get back to my normal self.

On another trip to Accra, I even got to meet and talk at length to the Rev. Jerimiah Wright. It was a delight to talk to him about a range of issues, including his travels through many parts of Africa. Yet my most memorable flight during that time was one of the turnaround flights to Lagos, Nigeria, on April 1, 2011. When my crew and I met in the lobby of the hotel, we looked around — everyone on the crew was Black. Immediately, a sense of pride and joy almost overwhelmed me. It was the very first time I ever had the awesome privilege of flying with an all-Black crew at United Airlines. We made sure to take plenty of photos to mark the historic occasion, but unfortunately, United Airlines management didn't care to give our little moment in Black history any publicity.

Regardless, we enjoyed every minute of this historic occasion because it was extremely rare to work a flight where everyone on the crew was Black. As a matter of fact, I had the opportunity to fly with the first Black captains at United Airlines when I was a copilot. I flew with Captain Bill Norwood and George Nixon when I was a 727 flight engineer. Also, I flew with Captain Jim Edwards when I was on the 747-400 as well. These legendary Black captains at United paved the way for other Black pilots like me who came along years later. In fact, I made it a point to take photos every time I got a chance to fly with a Black copilot. On the contrary, all-white crews had been the norm since the early days of the airline industry until they were forced to hire Black pilots and flight attendants. Obviously, discrimination in the airline industry was something that needed to be addressed.

Trying to Break Glass Ceilings into Management

IT'S REASONABLE TO assume no white pilot has ever had to file a lawsuit to get hired as an airline pilot. On the other hand, Black pilots have had to file lawsuits or appeal to government leaders in order to fly in the military or fly with commercial airlines. Sometime around 1941, the NAACP was instrumental in getting the government to allow Black men to fly, fight, and win. The heroic all-Black military flight units became known as the Tuskegee Airmen. After World War II was over, the Tuskegee Airmen found it difficult, if not impossible, to get hired at commercial airlines. They had no choice but to seek careers in fields other than flying. In the early 1960s, Marlon Green, a highly experienced Black Air Force pilot, applied at Continental Airlines and was turned down. He sued and his case ended up in the Supreme Court, where he won, and Continental Airlines was forced to hire him. In later years, commercial airlines began to hire one or two Black pilots here and there, while thousands of white pilots were being hired.

Because United Airlines was the largest airline in America in the '70s, the Equal Employment Opportunity Commission (EEOC) began to question why there were so few Blacks employed as pilots, managers, or other desirable positions at the airline. Unbeknownst to me, the EEOC investigation and subsequent litigation were ongoing when I first applied for a pilot job at United Airlines in 1985. After being turned down, I continued to apply for pilot jobs at American Airlines, US Airways, and Delta Airlines. In 1987, Congresswoman Cardiss Collins, together with Congressman John Conyers, challenged United Airlines' hiring practices for pilots, mechanics, and management positions. With the combination of litigation and legislative pressure, United Airlines and the EEOC agreed to a consent decree that led to me and many other Black pilots being hired in or around June 1988. It is noteworthy that I had no idea I had been recalled by United to be reinterviewed in 1987 because they were desperate to hire Black pilots to comply with the mandatory consent decree.

Of course, there was a backlash by several white pilots at United who started claiming that inexperienced Black pilots were taking jobs from white pilots. After hiring about two hundred Black pilots between 1987 and 1995, the EEOC agreed to dissolve the consent decree and United Airlines management gradually returned to hiring fewer Black pilots and limiting the number of Blacks particularly in flight management. Years later, around

2009, I noticed nearly all of the Black pilots in management at United that I knew were no longer there. That's when I sent a letter to CEO Glenn Tilton to make him aware of my experiences with racism at United and the lack of Black pilots in flight management. There was absolutely no reply to my letter.

Ironically, I wasn't the only person who noticed what seemed like a purge of Black pilots from the management ranks at United Airlines. A coalition of Black pilots that became known as the United Coalition for Diversity & Inclusion had been actively challenging United management to promote more Black pilots into management. Around the same time, United Airlines and Continental Airlines agreed to merge the two air carriers into one. It was understood that as the airlines merged, the few remaining Black pilots in management could probably be pushed out. Ultimately, we all came to the conclusion that if United was going to retain the Blacks in management or promote more Black pilots, it was up to us.

Because of my connections with the NAACP, I went to work in 2010 and successfully got a resolution passed entitled *In Support of More Diversity at United Airlines and Other Air Carriers*. Thanks to a coordinated effort, the coalition of Black pilots was hopeful that some of us would be seriously considered for a management promotion. Unfortunately, we got hoodwinked and bamboozled by some slick management tactics, and by some slick lawyers too. Even our own lawyers seemed to be working against us, making it virtually impossible to win. Furthermore, the top leadership at the NAACP is yet to follow through with the full intent of a binding resolution that pledged support. Nevertheless, I will always honor the 100+ year legacy of the NAACP organization that defiantly challenged lynchings and discrimination at a time when no one else cared enough. That's why I am still proud to say that I am a LIFE member of this historic civil rights organization.

Johnnie Edward "Jet" Jones Jr.

A staunch advocate for the advancement of Black pilots

I became consumed with overcoming the weight of world of institutional racism that had thwarted the upward mobility for Black pilots in the airline industry. The goal was to get enough support from congressional leaders, civil rights leaders, and litigators to convince airline management that our coalition of Black pilots was just as worthy of moving up through the management ranks as our white counterparts.

For a while, it seemed like the leadership of National Urban League was advocating for us, but soon that fell through too. The National Action Network and all other civil rights groups never responded to my letters asking for support. Needless to say, I was absolutely devastated by the sheer lack of concern or support by Black leaders and the overbearing efforts by our employer to defeat our mission. As an absolute insult, a few Black pilots who opted not to be a part of our coalition were tapped for low-level management positions. This, too, seemed like a clever, spiteful tactic used to give the appearance of management diversity. Ultimately, I finally came to realize that the EEOC seemed to be complicit in helping employers dismiss claims of discrimination and retaliation. That was when I also came to the stark and disturbing realization that the federal courts had started to intentionally shun discrimination litigation, and no one was willing to do what it took to help us break the glass ceiling and pathways between Black pilots and senior airline management. This time, I nearly broke down under the heavy weight of the world I found myself living in. Nothing made sense. Ultimately, it seemed nobody cared and my fervent prayers to God went unfulfilled. But soon the Serenity Prayer would eventually make sense. I came to accept that there are some things I cannot change no matter how hard I try. Nevertheless, I had the wisdom to know that it will take more time, effort and creative thinking for aspiring Black pilots to break through to senior management. Thus, another benefit from rejection is the motivation to explore starting a majority Black owned and operated airline so we don't have to beg white people for promotions to senior positions. We just create our own senior management positions at a successful airline that we own and control ourselves.

Thankfully, I had been able to read some very good self-help books that changed my life and allowed me to move to a higher level of consciousness. Two books in particular were *The Power of Now* and *The New Earth*, both by the brilliant author Eckhart Tolle. *The Power of Now* took me back to my early years in Americus when I would listen to a DJ named Doc Suttles on the only Black radio station in the area, which was in Albany, Georgia. When signing off at the end of his show, he would always say, "Life is hard by the yard, but it's a cinch by the inch." Ultimately, I came to understand the true meaning of this phrase, which is: take life one day at a time, and if life gets really hard, take life one second at a time. Why? Because it is always now, and this second is the only time that matters.

His other book, *The New Earth*, gives a vital lesson about how to recognize the ways the ego tricks us into avoiding the present moment, and how it makes us feel separated from other people, and God too. The most vital and useful lesson I learned from these books and a few others is that everything that happens has to happen. I also learned that real peace of mind comes from unconditional love and embracing our unbreakable spiritual connection with everyone and everything in the universe, and God too. Most of all, I learned that hate is a heavy burden that only love can overcome. Love conquers all.

Throughout the five years since the mandatory age sixty-five law forced me to retire from my beloved job as a commercial airline pilot, I have continued to apply for open non-flying positions at United Airlines. Being that I am a retired United Airlines captain with an unblemished record, you might think that I might be worthy of an interview. Yet and still, I have been repeatedly denied the opportunity to interview and have apparently been bypassed once again for positions that I seem to be completely qualified for. Could this be evidence of age discrimination, intentional illegal retaliation or could it merely be more motivation to start the Black owned airline to be called AFRICAMERICA AIRLINES? Regardless, I have no hard feelings or animosity towards anyone at United Airlines. I love that United Airlines gave me the awesome opportunity to enjoy a safe and prosperous thirty plus year career an airline pilot with seventeen great years as a captain. I do sincerely hope and pray that someday the courageous efforts of a few Black airline captains and others will be widely recognized for trying to awaken the consciousness of senior airline management. We risked it all as we boldly sought to open up pathways for some of us to move up through management just like Captain Marlon Green successfully sought to open a path to become an airline pilot in the early '60s. Nonetheless, we have a sacred duty and God given right to be defiant and fearlessly testify about our experiences challenging racial discrimination wherever it exists without fear or retribution or retaliation. On the bright side, the outright rejection led me to begin serious efforts to start AFRICAMERICA AIRLINES. I may never have come up with this bold idea if it had not been for those individuals who were absolutely determined to keep us outspoken Black airline pilots from moving up through the ranks to senior management. That's why I am at peace with whatever comes along.

The dramatic chain of events between 2012 and 2020 ultimately motivated me to write this book. Simply put, it would be unconscionable to depart this life without documenting some interesting occurrences that may help someone else overcome the burdens of life. As Fayette County NAACP president, I had been involved in a successful effort between 2012 and 2016 to bring district voting to my county despite fierce opposition from white leaders. Concurrently, I was part of the effort to break the management glass ceiling at United Airlines that was not so successful. Thus, the Serenity Prayer that I adore still rings true. Lastly, my two older sisters passed away in the middle of the last decade. After being ill for a while, my sister Linda left us in November 2013. Not long afterward in 2014, our oldest sister also passed away after her health declined.

When it comes to dealing with the death of family members or friends, there is an important paragraph in the book *A Course in Miracles Made Easy* by Alan Cohen. It essentially says death is not real; there's only life. It goes on to state that the universe has a way of using death to clear out what has served its purpose. The overall message is that in the face of death, we are forced to confront the mortality of the body. We must realize we are spirits and we need to probe deeply to find out who we really are and why we are here. In *The Power of Now*, Tolle describes death as the stripping away of all that is not you. He says you must die before dying to discover there is no such thing as death. This is why I find reading a wide array of books by intelligent or deep-thinking authors so satisfying.

While I continued my airline career, my marriage suffered immensely from my constant day-to-day coordination with coalition pilots trying to get vital support. After serving eight years as the Fayette NAACP branch president, I also came to the conclusion that the psychological damage inflicted upon my Black people as a whole during and after slavery was way too devasting to surmount in such a short time. Frankly, it sometimes seems Black people will never rise above all of the damage that has been done to our collective dignity, ambition, and self-respect.

At the local level, the NAACP volunteers who eagerly serve their communities are the unsung heroes that keep the organization viable. Nevertheless, my overall personal conclusion is that at the national level, the NAACP has lost a lot of credibility, and it is questionable whether anyone can rely on them to follow through on binding resolutions passed by the organization. Realistically, we have to acknowledge that egotistical white and even some Black people in high places have deliberately harmed or hindered the advancement of Colored, Negro, Black, African American people over the last four hundred years. Once I got to the point where I understood that taking on the weight of racism and the self-hate among my people was holding me down, I decided to step away from any serious involvement with the NAACP and essentially end my efforts to challenge the lack of diversity and inclusion for Black pilots.

Dr. Cornell West and Tavis Smiley are two well-known people

I got to meet while trying to address the woeful lack of diversity and inclusion of African Americans in airline management. These two brothers had the rare courage to question President Obama, and unlike many Black people, I understand why. I shall be forever grateful to have met these men and shared my story with them. Overall, I am ashamed to admit that my letters and appeals to the Obama administration for assistance countering racial discrimination against my fellow airline captains and I went nowhere.

The part of the Serenity Prayer that says, "God grant me the serenity to accept the things I cannot change" finally resonated with me. All things considered, Black people like me have managed to get some white people to change. Yet far too many white people have been silent or stood by and allowed racial bias to go on and on. Because of this, I managed to redirect my efforts to figuring out how I would serve out the remainder of my airline career. I had been assigned to the Dulles Airport on the 757/767 since the year 2000, and now I was nearing the mandatory retirement age of sixty-five. At one point, I thought I might be able to retire as a 787 Dreamliner captain, but I needed a good reason. The deciding factor was when United Airlines decided to start flying the 757-300 into Washington National Airport. The 757-300 is a long and clumsy version of that airplane and is very challenging to land on a short, seven-thousand-foot runway.

One night, I was working a flight from Denver to Washington National (DCA) in a 757-300 and we were assigned the River Visual Approach to runway 19. I had flown the River Visual to runway 19 at DCA before during the daytime, but at night that approach was always difficult and demanding. I had to follow the winding Potomac River while slowing and configuring the aircraft with flaps and landing gear as we descended at a sharp angle to the runway in order to avoid flying over or near heavily populated Washington, DC, and the monuments nearby. At about one thousand feet, the runway would finally become visible, and I had to bank that long, clumsy airplane hard to the right while focusing on the glide path indicators on the side of the runway.

My heart thumping, I managed to get lined up with runway 19 at five hundred feet, maintaining a safe approach speed of 145 knots, and touched down within the first thousand feet. After touchdown, the autobrakes kicked in and I put the engines in full reverse thrust to slow the airplane to taxi speed. That was when I realized that this kind of flying is for younger pilots, not me. I had previously met the challenge of flying into the most difficult commercial airports around the country, like LaGuardia Airport in New York City as well as San Francisco, Santa Anna, and San Diego in California. With about eighteen months before retirement in 2017, I began to look forward to going to training in Denver for the first time in seventeen years to learn how to fly the brand-new 787 Dreamliner.

Flying the Boeing 787 Dreamliner over the Atlantic

The 787 Dreamliner is one of the most advanced twin-engine wide-body commercial airliners ever built. Its most outstanding capability is its ability to fly faster and go farther than most other airliners. After completing 787 training in early 2018, I flew mostly from Washington Dulles to San Francisco, Denver, or London. The longest route out of Washington Dulles was to Beijing, which was a fifteen-hour flight over Russia and other remote areas. This flight required a captain and three first officers due to the long length of the flight. Because of all the bad things I had heard about China over the years, I really had no desire to fly to mainland China, which is vastly different from Hong Kong, where I enjoyed flying to. That was why I tried my best not to fly to Beijing, but there was one trip I couldn't get out of.

In May of 2018, I worked a flight to Beijing, which was my first, last, and only time going there. The layover was nearly two days long, so I got to see some of the city and went shopping with one of my copilots. The crewmembers who fly there loved to go shopping for cheap stuff made in China, but that didn't excite me. After going to the shopping district, we went to a strange place to get something to eat. There were pictures on the menu but nothing in writing that I recognized, so I had to select something that looked familiar. Whatever that was that I ate was horrible, and finding something good to eat was not easy.

On the bright side, I was able to connect with Shayna Marie Shaw, one of my wife's relatives living in China and teaching English to Chinese students. It was great having someone who could give me some insight into the Chinese culture. After we had dinner, I returned to my hotel to find other things to do on that long layover. Before leaving the United States, I knew getting on the internet to check my Facebook page and other social media sites required a lot of preparation. This was necessary because in

China, internet traffic is restricted or censored and a VPN (virtual private network) is essential.

Overall, I dreaded being there and couldn't wait to leave. I made the decision to never go back again, even though several trips to China were sometimes unavoidable in the bidding process. Usually, I could trade out of them or get out of them some other way. Just the thought of flying to China often made me feel sick, so there were times I called crew scheduling to be put on the sick list. After several sick calls, my Black chief pilot started hassling me about my use of sick leave. Fed up with his harassment, I sent him an email asking if he had ever heard anyone say, "You make me sick." I went on to tell him in so many words that harassment over the use of sick leave is unethical and a threat to the safe operation of the airline.

After that, around November of that year, I decided to have cataract surgery in the hopes of improving the vision in my left eye. Most unfortunately, my recovery from the cataract surgery did not go well and the vision in my left eye was adversely impacted. At first, I was resigned to the idea that I might never be able to fly the ceremonial final trip, where you taxi in after making that last landing and the firetrucks on each side create an arc of water signifying the end of a long, illustrious career. Once I realized it was possible to get an FAA waiver to fly again, I started jumping through the hoops and the slow regulatory process to get a waiver to hopefully get back in time to fly that last trip before my mandatory August 1, 2019, retirement date. As fate would have it, I got my FAA medical certificate on my retirement date, which ended what had been a heroic effort to try to end my thirty-two-year airline career with the fire-truck water-cannon salute as I had planned to.

I would be lying if I said I wasn't deeply disappointed. On the other hand, God gave me a wakeup call I will never forget. A longtime friend and fellow United Airlines pilot died from prostate cancer on my sixty-fifth birthday and retirement day after I had visited him a few days earlier. The disease weakened Dave, but he was in good spirits. We hadn't seen each other in a while, but we talked about old times and how we had been young Black pilots trying break through to the major airlines. Sensing he wouldn't be alive much longer, I gave him a copy of my poem entitled "Black Wings" and told him that I loved him as I prepared to leave his home bewildered and searching for the meaning of life. Dave's passing made me realize how abundantly blessed I was to still be alive and healthy enough to enjoy retirement. My resentment about not getting back to work in time to fly my retirement trip faded as I thought about how my friend Dave didn't even make it to his retirement day.

BLACK WINGS

I have lived the dream of sprouting black wings and roaring aloft into yonder blue skies. Rolling down the runways of life up through turbulent winds of change, I rise. Yes, I have overcome the drag of despair and the weight of this world to get in the air and do what I love; to fly like a mighty blackbird and be proven airworthy like the eagle or the dove.

Thrusting my way toward heaven, racing through space, I find peace in this place. Dare I ponder my plight as I endure the glory of flight; the spirit of God sustains me. So, it matters not where I fly for wherever I go, I always know he is the wind beneath my wings.

Now fulfilled with his grace I depart this airspace, idle my throttle and earthward I race. Down, down through clouds and crosswinds I skillfully navigate my craft on outstretched black wings of faith. Then gently I glide to a smooth landing with pride, I am a black aviator, blessed and forever dignified.

© John E. Jones 2002

Retirement and Beyond

THROUGHOUT MY AIRLINE career, I successfully passed every flight evaluation that all professional pilots are subjected to each year. Few airline pilots can match that record. Because I was so passionate about flying, I had the dedication to do whatever it took to become an expert at flying airplanes and choosing the best ones to fly. Most of all, I recognized that most of the time my landings were impressive because I made it a point to always stay focused on making smooth landings and letting God take care of everything else. On my pilot's license, I have what the Federal Aviation Administration refers to as type ratings on the Boeing 747/757/767/777 and 787.

Despite some serious problems in 2019 and 2020 with the 737 MAX, airplanes made by Boeing are some of the safest and best-designed aircraft ever built. Instinctively, I never had a desire to fly the 737 because unlike every other Boeing airplane, it has a small and cramped flight deck with an annoyingly noisy trim wheel that spins every time you trim the airplane. In my humble opinion, perhaps Boeing's decision to push the 737 well beyond its original design limits is what led to hundreds of people being killed in two separate crashes that occurred around the time of my retirement. The 757 is a far superior airliner, yet the 737 MAX is replacing it because it is cheaper to operate.

Me and Dave Harris not long before he passed away

An interesting series of events took place as I turned sixty-five, retired from United Airlines, and planned for my post-retirement life. I had planned my own retirement party for August 3, 2019, at the Sheraton Hotel on Camp Creek Parkway. Thankfully, I was able to get many people I have known for decades together to celebrate my retirement from forty-seven years of aviation. Folks from my Americus years, Air Force days, and Clark College days as well as family members had a great time and got to see me give my testimony about how I overcame the weight of the world many times. I am so grateful to have had the chance to have a retirement party to mark the beginning of a new era. Thereafter, several pilot friends came to Atlanta to attend what was an amazing homegoing and funeral for Captain Dave Harris. I was asked to recite my "Black Wings" poem, which is so befitting for recognizing the joy and pain of being a proud Black pilot. Captain Dave Harris left a great legacy as one of the few Black men who have not only been a pilot, but also a lawyer.

It was now time to figure out what to do next. Navigating my way through the Medicare maze was a nightmare and dealing with government incompetence really got to me. There were so many surprises to being retired and no one could have prepared me for what I had to deal with. Being that I had previously been the first vice president of the Georgia State NAACP, it was my intent to try one more time to become president of the organization. But, in October 2019, my run for Georgia State NAACP President was unsuccessful due to a chaotic election process and a lack of support. The outcome of that election helped me decide to move on from the NAACP and to explore other options.

In the meantime, I was able to plan a small reunion of airmen I had served with at Moody AFB in Valdosta way back in the '70s. Larry Henderson, Lewis Carswell, Donald Smith, Henry Bunn, Melvin Sessions, and I gathered at an airshow at Moody AFB in early November 2019. Thereafter, we got together at Big Nick's Restaurant, in Valdosta where we reminisced about old times, laughed, and talked late into the evening.

Johnnie Edward "Jet" Jones Jr.

Air Force buddies Lewis Carswell, Larry Henderson & me

Over the years, I have found that overcoming the weight of the world is and will always be a constant struggle. Retirement has essentially become a full-time job for me, and I find that it takes a lot of work to navigate my way through the maze. First, I had to start collecting on the PBGC pension that pays me about two-thirds what I would have gotten from my pension from United Airlines. The fact that selfish corporate executives cheated me out of my pension will always be a sore subject for me. After working for the better part of forty-seven years, it is not easy for me to not be working a job or running a thriving business. Unfortunately, no company has had an interest in hiring me, although I applied for several jobs with the FAA, the Air Force, Boeing, Gulfstream, General Electric, and other employers.

Since I had always wanted to develop my AFRICAMERICA business, I decided to take an event-planning class so I could plan a series of events in 2020. After finishing the class, it was time to focus on scheduling a Black History Month event on February 1st to test my abilities. I held the event at the Black-owned This Is It! event center. My focus was on honoring local Black people who made history in the Fayette County area. Due to lack of interest or poor planning on my part, the event was not as well attended as I hoped. After assessing the event, I decided not to do any more live events. Instead, I would revise my business plan and focus on promoting something I call BLACK HISTORY DAYS which is a creative way to celebrate Black history all year. Soon, word began to spread about a deadly virus designated as COVID-19, or the coronavirus, that was said to have originated in China.

By May 2020, the coronavirus had killed nearly one hundred thousand people and the stock market had tanked. I had to fire the company that had been managing my retirement funds because I lost confidence in its ability to keep my account from losing too much value. In the midst of the coronavirus pandemic, racial unrest sharply escalated when an eight-minute, forty-six-second video emerged showing a white Minneapolis police officer snuff the life out of a large Black man named George Floyd. The whole world was stunned and violence broke out in many large cities around the nation. The Black Lives Matter movement and the videotaped murder of George Floyd finally motivated more white people than I have ever seen to speak out about white supremacy. Ideally, influential white people would have taken proactive measures to help lift Black people up and provide a level playing field we deserve as if slavery and racism had never been allowed in America. On the other hand, why should they? Only when tragedy strikes do we Black people make demands that ought to be made every day. How sad!

In the midst of all of the racial animosity, I sought to capitalize on the rare combination of my airline experience and my civil rights experience. I wanted to see if I could find work as a consultant. First, I pitched the idea of evaluating airline and hotel services to provide valuable feedback to corporations. Next, I submitted a proposal to help airlines deal with unconscious racial bias to avoid race-related conflicts. Needless to say, those ideas went nowhere as well. All the while, the coronavirus kept getting worse, and the worst president America has ever had didn't have a clue how to deal with the virus or rising racial tensions.

In the year 2021 when I began writing this book, the Republican Party had become the single vilest organization. It willfully protects and preserves racial bias, and there's little desire or will to do anything meaningful about it. It is also extremely odd that so-called "conservatives" are actually staunch "liberals" when it comes to firearms. They fiercely oppose any reasonable effort to restrict or regulate guns. As a result, every person in America is unnecessarily exposed to the ever-present threat of deadly gun violence every day. Most of all, I am convinced that because the United States of America was built on a foundation of white supremacy, racism with all its consequences will always weigh on any Black or African American person who lives in this country.

As I was writing this, Donald Trump has refused to concede and move on from an election he has clearly lost. His refusal to concede the election and his promotion of the "Big Lie" claiming he lost because the election was rigged have been used to justify a slew of new laws in so-called red states that seek to disenfranchise Black and brown voters. Only God knows what the future holds. Trump has brought an almost unbearable toxicity to politics, and many of us look forward to a better life after he is gone.

But I have overcome the weight of the world by accepting the reality that everything that happens has to happen. You, too, can find peace in this very important revelation. Transcending religion and accepting realism is the pathway to spirituality and a must if one is to have total peace of mind. In reality, I had to become an Air Force pilot, and to do so all I had to do was follow God's guidance every step of the way. I also had to write this book so you could read it and know how to overcome the weight of the world too.

Establishing My Legacy

IN MARCH 2020, Promyse Karriah-Marie Johnson was born. She is my first great-grandchild, and because of the coronavirus it took a while before I got the chance to hold her. This book is also dedicated to her and all my descendants. In the words of Stevie Wonder, isn't she lovely? Overall, it is my hope that I shall be remembered for a legacy of reading, learning, achieving, teaching, inspiring, and loving people. I came into this world with a healthy dose of curiosity and a yearning to learn as much as I can, especially about human nature. Through learning, I figured out how to achieve my primary goal of becoming an Air Force pilot, among other things. Through my writings of poetry, and now this book, I am able to teach what I know so others can learn.

Hopefully, I can write other books that will help people transition from religion to realism to spirituality in order to find peace of mind in the midst of a troubled world. Perhaps I will be able to teach those who read my books how to defy ego and learn to love everybody in order to reduce the hate and violence we often see on the news. It is also my hope to continue to do something that will benefit the people of my hometown, Americus, Georgia. Ideally, I would like to move back there and run for mayor. Why? Even though Black citizens in my hometown have always outnumbered white citizens for as long as I can remember, the citizens have never elected a Black mayor. Wouldn't it be great if I become the first Black mayor?

Me in Americus to visit Americus High School

I am extremely proud that a young airline pilot and Americus native named Troy Jones, no known relation, has essentially replaced me at United Airlines. He is currently a 787 First Officer. In 2019, Troy and I had visited Americus High School along with Americus native and Air Force officer Christopher Brown to inspire students to become pilots or pursue a career in aviation. A third Black pilot from Americus is Michael Harris who has just begun flying for a regional air carrier called Endeavor. We hope to be an inspiration for many other young Black people especially in Americus for decades to come. Hopefully, this book will help accomplish this goal.

One can never forget the experience of growing up in a place like Americus. Because of Jim Crow segregation and the oppressive conditions we encountered growing up, we Black Americus natives will always have a strong bond with each other and a connection to our hometown. That's why a vital part of my legacy is being a part of an investment club currently comprised of successful men who grew up in Americus. We came together around 2013 to pool our money, invest in stocks to make more money, and provide scholarships to deserving students in need.

While we started out with twelve members, only six of us remain in the group. These members include John Jordan, Alvin Bowen, Will Grimes, Robert Freeman, Earnest Brown, Calvin Mansfield, and me. Former members are Marvin Boone and Terryle Butts. William "Junior" Bowens, Willie "Big Time" Boynton, Ross Cleveland and Marvin Boone are four members who passed away. Incidentally, they all were Vietnam combat veterans, and I am proud they were a part of the legacy of the Americus Investment Group. Earnest Brown also passed away unexpectedly in 2021. He was perhaps the most successful Black person to have grown up in Americus.

Most of all, these guys have helped me be part of a legacy of giving back through the scholarship effort each year. I even got to go back to Americus High School after forty-seven years and speak to students about being a pilot who grew up in Americus. It was a humbling experience to be back at the place where I could inspire others to follow their dreams. Furthermore, my lifelong friend Carolyn Melinda Merritt also provided the inspiration and encouragement for me to write this book. Her book *Merritt Magic* has a wonderfully magical spell to it that created the springboard for mine.

AFRICAMERICA is the term I created to encompass the four-hundred-year evolution of a people and culture that have over the years been known by the names Colored, Negro, Black, and African American. I was compelled to create the amazing red-black-and-green AFRICAMERICA Flag to give my people a beautiful symbol that represents us and our courageous struggle in America. As a part of my AFRICAMERICA business, one of the things I plan to do is develop the concept I call the African American Empire, which I created to be a major inspiration to Black people. The goal of this empire is to help Black people realize our economic power and to coordinate efforts to flex that power to improve our lives.

Other goals of AFRICAMERICA are to promote the celebration of BLACK HISTORY DAYS and to promote Black history events, cultural tourism, historic sites, or museums. Besides the ambitious goal of starting AFRICAMERICA AIRLINES, another alternative and optimistic goal I have is to organize group trips to Ghana and acquire my own Gulfstream 650ER jet to transport people to various destinations of historical or cultural significance in Africa and other places.

Lastly, there are two songs that inspire me as I near the end of my time here. "Dream of a Lifetime" by Marvin Gaye is a great song that sums up my life better than anything I have ever heard. "Going Up Yonder" by Ben Tankard is sung by John P. Kee, and this song reminds me of the thousands of flights I have flown, as well as the last flight we all must take.

Words of Wisdom

ALONG THE WAY, I have found that very few people I know are able to move from religion to realism to spirituality as I have. Why? Because wholeheartedly embracing spirituality is something you have to crave. First, you have to be insatiably curious about why religion has so much influence or control over so many people. Conversely, why do some people shun or disobey religious beliefs like Christianity and continue to do harm to one another? Has it ever occurred to you that the untamed ego could be the root of all evil? If you have a conscience, how can you not ask yourself how, or why? Why isn't there a more effective form of religion or an ideal belief system that benefits everyone? Why isn't there a universal belief system that everyone can accept and believe in?

Next, you have to crave knowledge in order to find wisdom. Wisdom has immeasurable value to improve the lives of people all over the world. Yet, it is sad that too few people seek or find wisdom because they fall victim to traditional beliefs, manipulation, or they're too busy or, perhaps, too fearful to question what they are told.

Therefore, my goal is to promote the transition from religion to realism and ultimately to spirituality as a method of getting you to utilize the brain God gave you to gain wisdom from within just as well as you gain from outside of yourself. Like God, the spirit is the lowest common denominator and is everlasting. Furthermore, I believe all humans—and everything in the universe—are connected through the air we breathe. Thus, this should be the basis for a new universal belief system that can transform the world over time.

I urge you to build close-knit family relationships, which form the foundation of a great society. Moreover, strive to love everyone regardless of how you feel about them, and never hate anybody. It takes too much energy to hate. Try to always do good, especially when no one is looking or listening. Always remember to do good, because when you harm anyone else, you harm yourself too. Embrace the Serenity Prayer and its meaning to life. Periodically notice your breathing to get into the present moment, especially when the weight of the world becomes too heavy.

For my fellow African Americans, know thy history and teach others to love Black people and love being Black. Accept that many Black people have serious hidden psychological damage. For those who may cause you harm, try to push aside your ego and forgive them, for they know not what they do. Always be careful and curious, question everything, and read for understanding. Make safety a number-one priority to avoid mistakes, accidents, or regrets. Take note of your choices; think through your options so you can decide confidently. Look for and recognize the all-powerful Holy Spirit that dwells within you and everyone else.

Many people are burdened under the weight of so-called "sin," and some feel God has forsaken them. Yet it is my belief that it is well within our power to forgive ourselves by realizing if everything that happens has to happen, how can there be any sin unless you put it in your mind? Remember that everything begins and ends in your mind. Only you can decide what enters your mind and what stays there. This is why a deep understanding of psychology and human nature is oh so vital to a balanced life.

Again, I urge you to understand the difference between religion and spirituality. It will put you well on your way to becoming wiser and more enlightened. Accept that everything that happens has to happen; this is the ultimate way to completely release you from sin and guilt that can unintentionally or intentionally come from entrenched religious doctrine, teachings or beliefs. Recognize that religion has an extremely clever way of using the fear of going to hell to scare you into believing so you will become a better person and motivated to be a faithful and committed member of a church. For some people, this can be just what it takes to change their behavior and lives for the better. For others, it can be a stepping stone to get you to someday go beyond religion, the fear of dying and going to hell and ultimately become purely a spiritual person. That should be your ultimate goal so you can go beyond any fears you may have to accomplish great things and inspire others like I have. Learn to cherish your family and friends, nurture fond memories, and visit places of your youth to remind yourself of how far you have come. Learn to look well beyond your lifetime so you can plan and promote generational wealth. Find that one positive thing you are passionate about and pursue it relentlessly. Because thoughts come and go, write down your goals, plans, and desires so you can review them often. If you really want something, write it down, be very specific, and keep it in a private place. Pray often for what you need and want without anticipation or expectation and it will likely show up.

Lastly, perhaps this book would never have been written if it weren't for the motivation provided by the embarrassing presidency of Donald Trump and the restricted mobility caused by the COVID-19 pandemic. As of the year 2021, the GOP or Republican Party seems to have lost its soul and become the Trump Party. Never in my entire life have I seen one man corrupt an entire political party and bring so much shame upon this country. Amazingly, about seventy-four million American voters apparently wanted this pathological liar to be reelected. That, my friends, is a serious wakeup call. For four years, most Americans have had the weight of the world on their shoulders due to the unparalleled incompetence and arrogance in the White House. In my opinion, the United States of America could never survive another term with Donald Trump as president.

When Trump accidentally was elected in 2016, I felt like God was teaching us a lesson for being apathetic about voting and neglecting to make sure the right people are elected to public office. It took an egotistical maniac being president and an out-of-control deadly coronavirus that has, to date, killed well over seven hundred thousand American people to wake enough people up to vote him out of office. So far, COVID-19 has infected six people I know. Four of them have died. Two of them, Martha Brown Durham and Larry Furlow, were my high school classmates. Both of them will be missed.

Nevertheless, I understand why COVID-19 had to happen. I probably would have found other things to do if I didn't have to stay home trying to avoid getting infected. So, I've managed to go with the flow of things that happen from day to day, always searching for meaning. In my search for meaning, there is one thing I have come to realize and act on. No one should ever vote for any candidate unless and until that candidate and their political party openly denounce racism, voter suppression, voter intimidation, police misconduct, racial injustice, and health insurance inequities. The bottom line is that voting for people who are working against your best interests and your people will only perpetuate your misery and suffering. And don't ever fall for that argument about Republicans being the ones who freed enslaved people and Democrats being racists and founders of the KKK. Remember: racism never really goes away. Over time, it just changes form—or political parties. Today, it's intuitively obvious that so-called "conservatives" seem to have eagerly embraced racism with open arms. Therefore, if you call yourself a conservative and ignore the racism your party promotes, protects, and condones, you are keeping America from being great.

Because the United States of America was so out of balance, enough voters were motivated to vote the Trump administration out of office in November 2020. Fortunately, Joseph R. Biden was sworn in on January 20, 2021, and the country slowly began to regain its balance. Nevertheless, President Biden's inauguration occurred just fourteen days after a violent mob, including Republican extremists and terrorists, stormed the US Capitol Building in Washington, DC. on January 6, 2021.

Please understand this: I simply cannot emphasize how close we came to our government collapsing under the weight of division caused by one unusually deranged, egotistical man. Aided by lies spread by Fox News and other irresponsible media outlets, Donald Trump nearly destroyed the America we knew before he became president. By the grace of God, millions of American people understood the necessity to vote for Joe Biden and Kamala Harris, our very first Black and female vice president. If you are one of those who voted for the Democratic candidates, you can be proud to have helped save America. Nevertheless, I cannot emphasize enough how important it is for Congress to pass new legislation that protects and preserves the unimpeded right to vote. If the right-wing extremist conservatives ever regain control of the government again, a second civil war or race riots are a real possibility. Therefore, take heed and never neglect your sacred right to vote. Democracy in these United States of America is very fragile, and so far, the Democratic Party seems to be trying to do what's necessary to bring about a spirit of cooperation, unity, fairness, and balance. Lastly, as we follow recent developments in the 2024 presidential race, remember that if God wants Kamala Harris to become president of the United States of America there is absolutely nothing that can stop it. In fact, I believe she is exactly the person this country needs to bring all of the racism and sexism to the surface so we can deal with it once and for all. Isn't that worth voting for? With Kamala Harris as president, America could enter a new era where it is possible to restore balance to a country where the toxicity of centuries of white supremacy has caused it to lean to far to the right far too long. On the other hand, a second Trump administration has the potential to be devastating and throw the country into chaos and disfunction. Most importantly, we must all be mentally prepared for either outcome. Why? Always remember that everything that happens has to happen and we as the old folks used to say we will understand it by and by.

This Do in Remembrance of Me

ALWAYS HAVE FAITH and never give up on life or God, or should I say the Holy Spirit! You are here for a reason. Embrace religion as a pathway to truth and, ultimately, realism and spirituality. If Christianity appeals to you, by all means study it and go to church to seek more understanding. But don't stop there. Most of all, never be satisfied with what you think you know or what you have been told. If you ain't learning, you ain't living right. You must become a *student for life*.

Always read the Bible and other books of interest and seek to find something that resonates with you. Learn how to interpret the many messages that come to you from various sources, just like I attempted to do with the number 232. Have faith in God, yourself, and your ability to find balance in a world that seems unbalanced. Reflect on the Twenty-Third Psalm and other meaningful scriptures, or any sentence in a nonreligious book that gives you hope.

Pass this book down to future generations so they can learn from it. Write your own story and give me credit for inspiring you. Accept God as a universal spirit—*US*—and always give thanks to the creator. As an example of my spiritual growth, especially since writing "Black Wings," I have begun trying hard to avoid referring to God as *He*. Why? Because God is so much greater than the image man has endeavored to give the spirit that cannot be seen but is readily felt. Instead, think of God as a magnificent omnipotent holy spirit that is within everyone and everything, and you will go beyond the limitations humankind tries to put on you and God.

Lastly, as you age over time, I suggest you mentally prepare yourself to face the inevitable health challenges that will creep up over time. Equip yourself, as I have, with as much knowledge as you can about how to care for the human body and stay healthy. Also, learn to accept whatever condition you cannot change. And when you're finally able to come to grips with your mortality, you will learn how not to worry about what lies beyond today or the end of your life. Then you can imagine the perfect peace that comes with being fearless. Only God alone knows the uncertain future, especially after this life, and that's what people fear. This is precisely why you must always strive to live in the present moment and watch your fears dissolve. How? Whether you're alive or dead, it will always be now, which is the only time that matters.

CONCLUSION

If you have ever needed proof that we are all dependent on one another, just reflect on my life. During my thirty-two-year career as a commercial airline pilot, hundreds of thousands of people relied on me to get them to their intended destinations. I am grateful I was able to accomplish that goal. Conversely, there are many people I depended on too. Specifically, my gratitude goes out to aircraft manufacturers like Boeing; aircraft engine makers Pratt & Whitney, Rolls-Royce, and General Electric; all of my flight instructors, aircraft mechanics, and air traffic controllers; and everyone else who contributed to my successful career as a pilot.

Aside from my professional career, I have depended on family and friends for support, and I supported them as well. I give a special tribute to people like the Rev. Ed Johnson, a retired Navy officer whom I worked closely with as we transformed Fayette County into a welcoming place for all people. Also, Attorney Wayne Kendall deserves special recognition for his extraordinary work challenging racism in Fayette County as well. My friend Mike Williams, too, has been an inspiration because of his outstanding achievements as an aeronautical engineer and successful business owner. Another influential person I want to mention is my HVAC technician, Harris McFerrin. Harris and I developed a unique friendship, and he inspired me to continue flying as a commercial airline pilot as long as I could. Moreover, I shall never forget the vast amount of wisdom and wit this man has to share to anyone willing to listen.

Johnnie Edward "Jet" Jones Jr.

Over the years, I had the privilege of having several famous people on my flights. After his term as president, former president George H. W. Bush was on one of my flights. On another flight, his wife Barbara was on board. Other famous passengers were Ramsey Lewis, Ron Brown, Don Cheadle, and Supreme Court Justice John Roberts. My most cherished memory is when Stevie Wonder flew on my flight from Washington to Las Vegas the day after the second inauguration of President Obama. Fortunately, I was able to take a photo with Stevie.

The story of my life is about overcoming the weight of the world to get in the air and do what I love and find peace of mind. Gravity is what holds us—and almost everything around us—down. I also learned that everything in the world, including you and me, needs balance. Airplanes need to be balanced, and the engines that propel them into flight also require balance. The ever-constant pursuit of balance requires an abundance of knowledge and wisdom that can only come from using the mind to absorb vital information.

By God's grace, I have accomplished many things that others

have only dreamed of. For example, how many people have flown solo in a jet aircraft thousands of feet in the air and been able to land it safely? My sweet cousin Pam Kendrick Fields, who just obtained a doctoral degree, recently revealed that she initially wanted to be an Air Force fighter pilot. Yet, she settled on being a distinguished educator and administrator in Americus instead. I, too, could have been something else, but I was able to tap into some mysterious power that defied the odds stacked against me. I was born Black into a family with meager means on the wrong side of town and raised by a struggling single parent with undiagnosed diabetes. In spite of my humble beginnings, I followed through on my lofty dreams to become a jet pilot. Somehow, I knew every door that slammed in my face caused a window to open elsewhere. When there was neither an open door nor a window for me to go through, I found a crack in the wall or the roof. Never did I let the idea of failure enter my mind.

In a jet airplane, when you are holding in position on the runway and the tower controller issues your takeoff clearance, you release the brakes and push the throttles up to the takeoff power setting. The jet engines roar to life, generating thousands of pounds of thrust as you begin to roll faster and faster down the runway. As you roll along, the wings generate the lift required to overcome the drag and weight of the world, and at the proper airspeed, you pull back on the flight controls and become airborne. That was what happened when I was just a child dreaming about becoming a jet pilot. I pushed up the throttles of my imagination, and everyone necessary to get me airborne became the engines that propelled me into the air. The rest is history.

My illustrious aviation career spanned over forty-seven years. All total, I have flown some twenty thousand hours in eight different kinds of aircraft. I have been to many parts of the world, and I am most grateful to have been able to fly to Mother Africa several times. Honestly, every Black or African American who can afford to visit Ghana or any African country where our enslaved ancestors came from should do so. If you do, you will be forever proud of those who survived horrific conditions in the belly of a smelly old slave ship so you could be born centuries later. It's the least you can do to honor their memory and sacrifices. Don't you agree? This is why I seriously began exploring the idea of starting a transatlantic Black-owned airline with an all–787 Dreamliner fleet called AFRICAMERICA AIRLINES. Using my college motto—find a way or make one— should and will give me the courage to continue to do great things.

Lastly, I consider myself to be a spiritual teacher nowadays, and I acknowledge that there is no such thing as death because I believe the spirit is everlasting. Thank you for picking up my book. I am blessed that you have had enough interest to read my amazing story. If you need to contact me while I am here, send me an email at thejetwillfly@gmail.com. I would love to know what, if anything, you might have learned from reading my book. Have I inspired you to put your story in writing? I certainly hope so. And lastly, if you have any constructive feedback, please feel free to let me know. Thanks!

ACKNOWLEDGMENTS

First and foremost, I acknowledge God and the Holy Spirit, which I also call the Universal Spirit (or US). God gave us a mind to figure things out, so I wrote this book to let others know what I have been through in life and what I think about my journey. In my opinion, we all live in what I have come to call a perfect world. Better yet, I believe we live in a perfect universe that is always evolving. In spite of all the ups and downs we go through, we and everything in the universe are cyclical and always seeking a balance. By the grace of God, I have lived an exciting life and have survived multiple near-death experiences over a span in excess of sixty-nine years, which has allowed me the opportunity to publish this book.

I know without a doubt the Holy Spirit sustains me and protects me from day to day. Thankfully, my Christian religion has given me the curiosity to probe deeper into why people believe in whatever faith or religion they choose to accept. I have learned that fear can be paralyzing, which is what keeps many people from questioning things that may seem odd, mysterious, or unexplainable. As I delved deeper into Christianity, it became evident to me that Jesus Christ was presented to us as an example to follow and to learn from. Through my study of Jesus, I learned that love is the most powerful force known to mankind. Most notably, I believe it's not enough to simply believe in Jesus or whatever religion you choose; you must become like Jesus and love your fellow man or woman unconditionally in order to find love. In other words, I also believe you actually have to learn to love everybody regardless of who they are or what they do in order to receive the blessings of God. Why? Because we're all connected, and the love you give returns back to you.

Furthermore, you have to be able to forgive as well. It is essential that you have the innate ability to interpret or read between the lines to really understand the true purpose of religion so you can hopefully transcend religion and fully embrace the peace and tranquility of spirituality. Finally, I believe the Universal Spirit—or US—is the collective spirit of every living soul united by the air we breathe. Yes, that means every living being is connected by the air we all breathe, and love is the driving force that holds everything together.

Lastly, I humbly acknowledge my three sons, Curtis Bernard Wright, Johnnie Edward Jones III and Marion Alexander Jones, their children and future generations yet unborn. You are all challenged to live your lives with love and the utmost dignity. Use this book to help you and others to understand life and how to overcome the burdens that will come along in life. Remember that old familiar phrase inspired by Biblical scripture that says God will not put on you more than you can bear.

My sons Johnnie III, Curtis, Marion Alexander and myself

RECOMMENDED READING

Jet Pilot and Jet Pilot Overseas by Henry B. Lent

The Road Less Traveled by M. Scott Peck

Succeeding Against the Odds by John H. Johnson

Historical and Cultural Atlas of African Americans by Molefi K. Asante and Mark T. Mattson

The Debt by Randall Robinson

Power vs. Force by David R. Hawkins

The Laws of Thinking by Bishop E. Bernard Jordan

Divided Soul by David Ritz

How to Have Confidence and Power in Dealing with People by Les Giblin

You'll See It When You Believe It by Wayne Dyer

Be Who You Want, Have What You Want by Chris Prentiss

The Power of Now by Eckhart Tolle

The New Earth by Eckhart Tolle

Think and Grow Rich: A Black Choice by Dennis Kimbro and Napoleon Hill

Leveraging the Universe by Mike Dooley

Post Traumatic Slave Syndrome by Dr. Joy DeGruy

Black Labor, White Wealth by Dr. Claud Anderson

Hypnotic Writing by Joe Vitale

Maximum Influence by Kurt W. Mortensen

Manifesting Made Easy by Jen Mazer

A Course in Miracles Made Easy by Alan Cohen

A Return to Love by Marianne Williamson

You Are What You Believe by Hyrum W. Smith

Merritt Magic by Melinda Merritt

The Devil You Know by Charles Blow

White Fragility by Robin DiAngelo

How to Get Your Boss to Work for You by Faye Hardaway

ABOUT THE AUTHOR

Johnnie Edward Jones Jr. is an ambition man from Americus Georgia who rose from poverty to become a successful military and airline pilot as well as a distinguished leader and civil rights activist. Raised as the youngest of six by a single parent housekeeper during the latter days of the civil rights era, Johnnie defied the odds and used his service in the United States Air Force as a springboard for a promising career in aviation.

Through sheer determination, Johnnie developed a bold eight-year plan to help his ailing mom and prepare for the rigorous yearlong undergraduate pilot training course. He served four years as an active-duty T-38 and F-4E aircraft mechanic in the Air Force and used his GI benefits to get a bachelor's degree from Clark College. After graduating from Clark, Johnnie completed Air Force Officer Training School and started pilot training in March 1981. On March 18, 1982, he was awarded an aeronautical certificate and began his career as an Air Force Reservist pilot flying the C-130 Hercules, and ultimately flew the Boeing 747/757/767/777/787 at United Airlines. He retired in 2019 after accumulating over fifteen thousand hours flying around the world and spending over thirty years at United Airlines as a flight officer.

Aside from his successful airline career, he found the time to serve his community. His inspiration from participating in the civil rights movement as a child led him to become a dynamic local NAACP leader in Fayette County Georgia. Johnnie is proud to have created the term AFRICAMERICA to represent the Colored, Negro, Black, African American people, and their unique cultural experience in America. He resides in the Atlanta, Georgia area and is laying the groundwork for what he calls AFRICAMERICA AIRLINES to provide airline service between the United States and the African continent.

www.ingramcontent.com/pod-product-compliance
Lightning Source LLC
Chambersburg PA
CBHW050223100526
44585CB00017BA/1872